Hugo's Simplified System

Turkish in
Three Months

Hugo's Language Books Limited

Written by

Bengisu Rona BA (Istanbul), PhD (London)

Lecturer in Turkish Studies
School of Oriental & African Studies
University of London

Set in 10/12 Plantin by
Typesetters Limited
16, Mead Business Centre, Mead Lane, Hertford
Printed and bound in Great Britain
by Courier International Ltd,
Tiptree, Essex

Preface

'Turkish in Three Months' is a straightforward introduction to the essentials of the language and is primarily intended for those working on their own, or with a teacher for one or two hours a week. It could also serve as the textbook for a 15 or 20-session class course. The author is an experienced teacher of Turkish as a foreign language, now lecturing at SOAS, University of London. She's also Moderator in Turkish for GCE 'A' level and GCSE, London and E. Anglian Group.

The book begins with an explanation of Turkish pronunciation, as far as this is possible in print. Turkish spelling is much more regular than English and you will quickly learn to associate the written words with their sound. Using the book together with our audio cassettes is an ideal combination and provides another dimension to the course.

It has always been a principle of the Hugo method to teach only what is really essential. We assume that the student wants to learn Turkish from a practical angle, so the lessons contain those rules of grammar that will be of most use in this respect. Constructions are clearly explained and the vocabulary is both practical and up-to-date. Each lesson includes exercises to check your understanding, and the order in which everything is presented takes into account the need for rapid progress. The Conversation and Reading passages offer examples of everyday Turkish, covering topics such as shopping, sightseeing and booking a hotel room. Translations of these passages, together with answers to the exercises, are given at the end of the book.

Ideally, you should spend about an hour a day on your work (slightly less, maybe, if you've not bought the audio cassettes), although there is no hard and fast rule on this. Do as much as you feel capable of doing; don't force yourself, but learn well a little at a time. Before beginning a new section or lesson, spend ten minutes revising what you learned the day before.

When the course is completed, you should have a very good understanding of the language – more than sufficient for holiday or business needs, and enough to lead quickly into an examination syllabus if required. We hope you enjoy 'Turkish in Three Months', and we wish you success in your studies.

Contents

6

Lesson 1

1 The Turkish alphabet

The Turkish alphabet has 29 letters: 8 vowels and 21 consonants. It is the vowels which differ most from English sounds.

A a, B b, C c, Ç ç, D d, E e, F f, G g, Ğ ğ, H h, I ı, İ i, J j, K k, L l, M m, N n, O o, Ö ö, P p, R r, S s, Ş ş, T t, U u, Ü ü, V v, Y y, Z z

2 Pronunciation of vowels

(The English words cited as a guide to pronunciation are as in the Standard English of Southern England.)

a   as the 'u' in 'bun': **bak** 'look', **adam** 'man', **at** 'horse'

e   as in 'test': **kes** 'cut', **ev** 'house', **et** 'meat'

i   as in 'sit': **bin** 'thousand', **iki** 'two', **it** 'push'

ı   roughly like the -er combination in some English words, eg. 'letter', 'speaker': **kız** 'girl', **ısı** 'heat', **kıt** 'scarce'

ö   like the vowel in 'bird' or 'dirt' but short: **dört** 'four', **göz** 'eye'

o   as in 'pond': **on** 'ten', **oda** 'room', **ot** 'grass'

ü   as in the name of the German town 'Lübeck'; to produce this sound, the position of the jaw and the tongue is the same as for the articulation of the **i** sound, but the lips are rounded and pushed well forward: **ün** 'fame', **gül** 'rose', **büyük** 'big'

u   as in 'pull': **su** 'water', **bul** 'find'

3 Pronunciation of consonants

b   as in 'big', 'bad': **ben** 'I', **bak** 'look', **buz** 'ice', **biz** 'we'

c   like the 'j' in 'jam': **acı** 'bitter', **can** 'life, soul' ç   like the 'ch' in 'church': **üç** 'three', **aç** 'hungry', **saç** 'hair'

d   as in 'did', 'do': **dün** 'yesterday', **dokuz** 'nine'

f   as in 'fat', 'effort': **fil** 'elephant', **fark** 'difference'

palatalized with front vowel

g   as in 'get', 'goose': **git** 'go', **genç** 'young'

ğ   this letter (called **yumuşak g** or 'soft g') has no distinct pronunciation; it generally serves to lengthen the vowel before it: **ağ** 'net' is pronounced just as a long **a**, **doğru** 'correct' is **d** + long **o** + **r** + **u**. It does not occur at the beginning of a word.

h   as in 'how': **hiç** 'none', **hasta** 'ill', **hoş** 'pleasant'

j   like the 's' in 'measure', 'leisure': **ruj** 'lipstick', **garaj** 'garage'

palatalized with front vowels

k   as in 'kitten': **kent** 'city', **ilk** 'first', **kan** 'blood', **kuzu** 'lamb'

l   as in 'lily', 'lorry', 'all': **bil** 'know', **el** 'hand', **bülbül** 'nightingale', **göl** 'lake', **al** 'take', **ulus** 'nation', **kol** 'arm', **ılık** 'warm'

m   as in 'man': **masa** 'table', **mum** 'candle', **göm** 'bury', **müzik** 'music'

n   as in 'no': **ne** 'what', **niçin** 'why', **anla** 'understand', **on** 'ten'

p   as in 'pen': **perde** 'curtain', **pul** 'stamp', **küpe** 'ear-ring', **kapı** 'door'

r   The **r** is rolled between two vowels: **ara** 'interval', **arı** 'bee', **kuru** 'dry', **sürü** 'herd', **iri** 'big'. At the beginning of a word it is less prominent: **resim** 'picture', **renk** 'colour', **ruh** 'spirit'. At the end of a word it is always fully pronounced, with the exception of a few words that are frequently used, like **bir** 'one', where, in colloquial speech, it may not be heard at all. When fully pronounced at the end of a word, it has slight friction: **kar** 'snow', **duvar** 'wall', **vur** 'hit', **ver** 'give'.

very front in mouth

i.e. slightly less front

s   as in 'sea', 'decide': **eski** 'old', **son** 'final', **sis** 'fog', **üst** 'top', **askı** 'hanger'

ş   like the 'sh' in 'sheep', 'ash': **şu** 'that', **taş** 'stone', **iş** 'work', **kış** 'winter'

t   as in 'tea': **at** 'horse', **et** 'meat', **Türkçe** 'Turkish' (language), **kötü** 'bad'

v   as in 'vision': **var** 'there is/are', **ver** 'give', **kova** 'bucket' y   as in 'yes': **yıl** 'year', **yol** 'road', **uyku** 'sleep', **köy** 'village'

z   as in 'horizon': **zil** 'bell', **bez** 'cloth', **çöz** 'solve', **toz** 'dust', **uzun** 'long'

The English letters q, x and w are not found in the Turkish alphabet. The x sound is written as **ks** in some words taken from other languages: **taksi** 'taxi' and **ekspres** 'express'.

Rules for punctuation are much as in English. When a proper noun takes a case suffix, an apostrophe is put before the suffix: **İstanbul'a** 'to Istanbul', **Londra'da** 'in London'.

The circumflex accent is now very sparingly used. It makes the vowel on which it sits more front (see section 5 below) and the preceding consonant palatal. In writing it is retained in only a few words like **kâr** 'profit' as opposed to **kar** 'snow', and **bekâr** 'single, unmarried'. It causes the **k** sound in **kâr** to be palatalised – that is, to be followed by a slight y sound: **bekâr** is pronounced **'bekʸar'**.

4 Vowel length and vowel loss

Turkish vowels are short, except

1 when, in writing, a vowel is followed by ğ. Examples:

dağ, yağmur, ağaç, sağ, sığ

In all these examples the vowel before **ğ** (**yumuşak g**) is pronounced long.

2 in some words which are not Turkish in origin and still retain their long vowels. Examples:

tesir (**e** is long) 'influence'; **beraber** (**a** is long) 'together'

A very limited number of words ending in consonants drop the vowel in the last syllable when they take a suffix (see section 5 below) that begins with a vowel. If the suffix begins with a consonant, there is no change to the basic word:

resim 'picture':	**resme** 'to the picture' (the vowel **i** is dropped)
	resimler 'pictures' (the vowel **i** is retained)
şehir 'town':	**şehre** 'to the town'
	şehirden 'from the town'

oğul 'son':	**oğlu** 'his son'
	oğulları 'his sons'
burun 'nose':	**burnu** 'his nose'
	burundan 'from the nose'

5 Vowel harmony

In Turkish, words and grammatical features are built up by means of suffixes (endings which are added to words). Some of these (inflectional suffixes) have a purely grammatical function; others (derivational suffixes) help to build up the vocabulary of the language by deriving new words from existing ones. For example, in English, 'I did not work' is a sentence consisting of four words. But it is expressed in Turkish by just one word: **çalışmadım**.

Çalış is the verb meaning 'work'; **-ma** puts the verb into the negative ('not'); **-dı** indicates that it is in the past tense ('did'), and **-m** shows that the subject of the verb is the first person, 'I'.

Similarly, 'I did not see' is **görmedim: gör** 'see', **-me** 'not', **-di** 'did' and **-m** 'I'. An extreme example of adding a string of suffixes to a word is

Değiştiremediklerimizden misiniz?
Are you one of those whom we were unable to change?

Another such example is

Avrupalılaştıramadıklarımızdan mısınız?
Are you one of those whom we could not Europeanise?

In these examples, you will have noticed that the first has a succession of **e** and **i** vowels, and that the second consists mostly of **a** and **ı** vowels. This is because the base of the first example, **değiş** ('change'), contains **e** and **i** sounds (front vowels), and the last vowel, **i**, determines that the vowel in the first suffix which follows is of the same type: **i** rather than **ı**. And the vowel in the first suffix determines the vowel in the next suffix, and so on. The vowel of each suffix is determined by the vowel which precedes it.

The base word of the second example, **Avrupa** ('Europe'), contains **a** and **u** sounds (back vowels). The last of these vowels, **a**, determines that the vowel in the first suffix is also a back vowel: **ı** rather than **i**. And this back vowel in its turn determines that the subsequent vowel is again a back vowel: **a** rather than **e**.

This feature is called vowel harmony. It is basically a stringing together of vowels of similar quality, so that there is a sound harmony extending over the whole word. Vowel harmony operates on two qualities of the vowels: whether they are back or front and whether they are round or non-round.

Back and front vowels

Turkish has eight vowels. Four of them are front vowels: **e, i, ö, ü**. These front vowels are produced with the tongue forward in the mouth: the middle-to-front portion of the tongue is raised towards the front of the roof of the mouth (although it does not touch the roof of the mouth).

The other four are back vowels: **a, ı, o, u**. The back vowels are produced with the front part of the tongue held low in the front of the mouth, while the back part of the tongue is raised towards the back of the roof of the mouth. When you make these sounds, it feels rather as if the front vowels are produced in the front of the mouth, and as if the back vowels are produced in the back of the mouth.

If the last vowel of the base (the main part) of the word is a front vowel, then the vowel in a suffix added to it will also be front, the vowel in each subsequent suffix being governed by the vowel of the syllable that precedes it:

el hand.   **ellerinde** in his hands

But if the last vowel of the base is a back vowel, then the vowel in the suffix which follows it will also be back, and the vowel in each subsequent suffix will again be determined by the vowel preceding it:

oda room   **odalarımızdan** from our rooms

There are some suffixes which are non-harmonic – that is, they always have the same vowel, regardless of the vowel in the preceding syllable.

Round and non-round vowels

The same eight vowels can also be grouped differently as round and non-round vowels. The round vowels are those we say with the lips rounded and slightly forward: **o, ö, u, ü**. The other four vowels are non-round: **a, e, ı, i**.

If the last vowel of the base of the word is a non-round vowel, then the vowels in the suffix which follows will also be non-round:

zengin rich   **zenginlik** richness (i.e. wealth)

If, however, the last vowel of the base is round, the inherent nature of the vowel in the *suffix* determines whether or not it harmonises with the round vowel in the base.

As far as vowel harmony is concerned, there are three kinds of suffix:

a) those in which the vowel is either **a** or **e**, and therefore can never be round, regardless of whether or not the vowel of the preceding syllable is round;

b) those in which the vowel can be **i**, **ı**, **u** or **ü**. If the suffix is of this type, the vowel will be **i** or **ı** if the preceding vowel is non-round, and **u** or **ü** if the preceding vowel is round;

c) those that do not harmonise at all with the final vowel of the preceding syllable (non-harmonic suffixes).

Some examples:

-DE is a suffix meaning 'in', 'on' or 'at'. The vowel in this suffix can be either **a** or **e** (**a/e** type, as in (a) above), so it can never be round.

ev house   **ev + -de**: **evde** in the house

The only vowel in the base is **e**. It is a front vowel, so the vowel in the suffix **-DE** is also a front vowel: **e**, giving the word **evde**.

kutu box   **kutuda**

The last vowel in the base is **u**, a back vowel, so the vowel in the suffix **-DE** will also be back. As the only two possibilities for this particular suffix are **e** (front vowel) and **a** (back vowel), the suffix for **kutu** is **-da**: **kutuda**

-Lİ is a suffix meaning 'with', 'containing', 'having in it'. This suffix belongs to category (b) above: its vowel can be **i**, **ı**, **u** or **ü**. Thus:

biber 'pepper': The last vowel in **biber**, **e**, is a front vowel – and it is also non-round. So the vowel in the **-Lİ** suffix will also be a front, non-round vowel when it is added to **biber**: **biberli** 'with pepper'.

ağaç 'tree': The last vowel in **ağaç**, **a**, is a back non-round vowel. So the vowel in the **-Lİ** suffix will be the one vowel out of the four possibilities (**ı**, **i**, **u**, **ü**) which is also a back, non-round vowel –

ı: **ağaçlı** 'with trees', 'wooded'.

süt 'milk': **ü** is a front, round vowel, so the vowel in the suffix will also be a front, round vowel: **sütlü** 'with milk'.

yağmur 'rain': The final vowel **u** is a back, round vowel, so the suffix vowel will also be a back, round vowel: **yağmurlu** 'rainy'.

Vowel harmony looks a little complicated at first, but you will find it quickly becomes instinctive. The chart below may help to summarise it:

Final vowel in the base	Suffix	
	type (a)	type (b)
a or **ı**	**a**	**ı**
e or **i**	**e**	**i**
o or **u**	**a**	**u**
ö or **ü**	**e**	**ü**

These are the descriptive labels for the eight Turkish vowels:

a:	back, non-round	**o**:	back, round
e:	front, non-round	**ö**:	front, round
ı:	back, non-round	**u**:	back, round
i:	front, non-round	**ü**:	front, round

6 Consonant changes

The process whereby a Turkish word is built up by adding suffixes with particular meanings or grammatical functions to the base of the word also brings about changes in the consonants. These occur at the point where the base and the suffix meet, or where one suffix is added to another.

1   When the base ends in one of the voiceless consonants

p, t, k, ç, s, ş, f, h

and it is followed by a suffix beginning with the letters **d, g** or **c,** then these three consonants become **t, k** or **ç** respectively. In other words, the initial consonant of the suffix also becomes voiceless when it follows one of the voiceless consonants.

For example, the **-DE** suffix we saw earlier (meaning 'in', 'on' or 'at': see section 5) will begin with either **t** or **d,** depending on the final consonant of the base:

ipte on the rope	but	**evde** in the house
sokakta in the street		**odada** in the room
yamaçta on the slope		**duvarda** on the wall
beşte at five		**çayda** in the tea
cepte in the pocket		

2 With very few exceptions, Turkish words do not end in the voiced consonants **b, d, g** or **c.** But Turkish does have a large number of words that are not verbs of which the *base* ends with **b, d** or **c.** Some of these words are Turkish in origin: many are borrowed from other languages (particularly Arabic and Persian).

These voiced consonants appear when a suffix beginning with a vowel is attached to the base. The Turkish for 'my' (the first person possessive suffix: see section 43) is **-(İ)M** (**-m** after a vowel: **-im, -ım, -üm** or **-um** after a consonant). Thus:

hesabım my bill	**armudum** my pear
yurdum my homeland	**senedim** my voucher
ağacım my tree	**ihtiyacım** my need

But when these words do not have a suffix, or are followed by a suffix beginning with a consonant, then the final voiced consonant of the base changes to **p, t** or **ç** – that is, it becomes unvoiced. Thus:

hesap bill	**hesaplar** bills
yurt homeland	**yurtlar** homelands
ağaç tree	**ağaçlar** trees
armut pear	**armutlar** pears
senet voucher	**senetler** vouchers
ihtiyaç need	**ihtiyaçlar** needs

3 A number of words have a base ending with the voiced consonant **g** following another consonant. The **g** appears when a suffix beginning with a vowel is added, but changes to the unvoiced consonant **k** when the word has no suffix, or when a suffix beginning with a consonant is added. Thus:

rengim my colour	but	**renk** colour
		renkler colours

When a word of more than one syllable which is not a verb ends with a vowel followed by the unvoiced consonant **k**, the **k** is changed to **ğ** when a suffix beginning with a vowel is added:

ayak foot   but   **ayağım** my foot
ayakta on foot
sokak street   **sokağım** my street
sokakta in the street

Although this **k** to **ğ** change does also occur in some one-syllable words, like

çok much/many   **çoğu** most of it

most retain the **k**, regardless of the fact that a vowel follows:

yük load   **yüküm** my load   .   **yükler** loads
ok arrow   **okum** my arrow   **oklar** arrows

7 Stress

Turkish words are often lightly stressed on the last syllable.

güzél   **açík**

Most place names, however, are stressed on the first syllable:

Ánkara   **Bódrum**
İzmir   **Mármaris**

but there are some exceptions:

İstánbul   **Edírne**
Diyárbakır   **Kastámonu**
Antákya   **Amásya**
Antálya

(Note the stress on **İstanbul** is different from the stress normally used by English speakers.)

Some grammatical forms push the stress to the syllable preceding them. The syllable before the negative suffix **-ME** (see section 32), for instance, is usually stressed:

bekleyémiyorum I cannot wait
konúşmuyor she is not speaking

When these grammatical forms are introduced, listen carefully to their pronunciation on the cassettes if you have them.

Exercise 1

Practise pronouncing the following words:

deniz sea	**çay** tea
otel hotel	**halı** carpet
araba car (originally a cart)	**arkadaş** friend
uçak aeroplane	**büyük** big
otobüs bus	**küçük** small
tren train	**açık** open
öğrenci student	**kapalı** closed
öğretmen teacher	**dolu** full
şarap wine	**boş** empty
kahve coffee	

Exercise 2

Put the **-DE** *suffix after the following words.*
For example: **deniz** (sea) – **denizde**
otel, araba, uçak, otobüs, tren, çay, kahve, halı, şarap

Exercise 3

Put the **-Lİ** *suffix after the following words.*
Example: **süt** (milk) – **sütlü**

şeker sugar	**koku** smell, scent
limon lemon	**para** money
tuz salt	**telefon** telephone
biber pepper	**numara** number
et meat	**kum** sand

8 Some greetings and basic phrases

The following list of commonly used greetings and basic phrases will help you to consolidate your pronunciation. If you have the cassettes, first listen to them, then read them out aloud, then listen again.

Günaydın. Good morning.
İyi akşamlar. Good evening.
İyi geceler. Good night.

There is no set expression for 'good afternoon', but you can say: **İyi günler**. Good day(s). This is an all-purpose greeting which can be used at any time during the day as a greeting, and also when taking leave of someone.

Allahaısmarladık. (colloquial pronunciation is '**alaasmaldık**')
Goodbye. (said by the person who is leaving)
Güle güle. Goodbye. (said by the person who stays behind)

Teşekkür ederim. Thank you.
Teşekkürler. Thanks.
Çok teşekkür ederim. Thank you very much.
Çok teşekkürler. Many thanks.
Response: **Bir şey değil.** It is nothing. Or **Rica ederim.** Not at all.
(lit. 'I request, beg'.)

It is not unusual for people to use these two expressions together:
Bir şey değil, rica ederim. or **Rica ederim, bir şey değil.**

Sağol. Thank you. (more informal than **teşekkür ederim**)
Lütfen. Please.

Nasılsınız? How are you?
Response: **İyiyim, teşekkür ederim.** I am fine, thank you.

And you immediately follow this up by asking in turn:
Siz nasılsınız? (And) how are you?
Response:
Ben de iyiyim, teşekkür ederim. I too am well, thank you.

Özür dilerim. I am sorry. (lit. 'I apologise'.)
Response: **Rica ederim.** Not at all.

Affedersiniz. Excuse me.
This is mostly used to begin a request:
Affedersiniz, müze nerede? Excuse me, where is the museum?
Müsaade eder misiniz! Excuse me (used mostly when you are trying to make your way through a crowd; lit. 'Would you allow (me)?')

Buyurun (often pronounced '**buyrun**') is a very common expression. It has several meanings:
1 'Yes?' as a response to **Affedersiniz,** if the person pauses for your response;
2 In shops and restaurants, to ask customers what they want;

3 'Come in' when there is a knock on the door;
4 'Here you are' when you are handing over something;
5 'Go ahead' when you give way to someone at a door, or in response to a request to take something.

evet yes
hayır no
peki OK, all right
tamam OK, that's it, that's right, that's fine
Çok güzel! Very nice! Lovely!
tabii of course

Geçmiş olsun. May it pass. (to indicate your sympathy when someone is ill or has an accident)
Başınız sağolsun. (lit. 'May your head be alive/healthy': to commiserate with someone over a death)
Yazık! What a pity! What a shame!

Elinize sağlık. Health to your hands. (to praise someone's cooking)
Response:
Afiyet olsun. May it be good for you.

Apart from being the set response when one's cooking is praised, this is said at the beginning of a meal to indicate that people can start eating, or when the meal is over.

Şerefe! Cheers!   Response: **Şerefe!** Cheers!

Hesap lütfen. The bill, please.
Üstü kalsın. Keep the change.

Efendim is a very frequently used expression with several meanings:
1 It is a form of address for people of either sex, rather like 'sir/madam': **Peki efendim.** 'Yes sir/madam'.
2 With a questioning intonation it means 'I beg your pardon?'
3 When answering when one's name has been called or answering the telephone, it means 'yes'.

İnşallah, 'God willing', is an expression used when you hope something will happen, as if this expression will prevent things from going wrong.

Lesson 2

9 Nouns and adjectives

Turkish nouns, like English ones, do not have any gender distinction –
that is, they do not fall into the masculine, feminine and neuter
categories seen in some languages. There are no rules of agreement
between an adjective and the noun it describes. Adjectives come before
nouns.

uzun long, tall (person)
saç hair   **uzun saç** long hair
kısa short
ders lesson   **kısa ders** short lesson
temiz clean
örtü cloth, cover   **temiz örtü** clean cloth
kırmızı red
palto coat   **kırmızı palto** red coat

Most adjectives can be used as nouns, when they indicate a person or
thing possessing the quality of the adjective.

Kırmızı temiz. The red one is clean.
Küçük ucuz, büyük pahalı. The small one is cheap, the big one is
   expensive.
Genç çalışkan. The young person is hard-working.

10 bir: indefinite article/numeral

The numeral **bir** 'one' is also the indefinite article 'a', 'an' in Turkish:
bir masa 'one table' or 'a table', **bir palto** 'one coat' or 'a coat'. When
there is an adjective before the noun, **bir** can come either before the
adjective or between the adjective and the noun:

1 **bir kırmızı palto** one red coat
2 **kırmızı bir palto** a red coat

When **bir** comes after the adjective and before the noun, it generally stands for the indefinite article, as in example 2 above. Other examples:

büyük bir otel a large hotel
temiz bir araba a clean car
kısa bir halı a short carpet

There is no definite article in Turkish: **ev** means 'house' or 'the house' depending on the context (but see section 34: **-(Y)İ**, definite object).

11 Plural of nouns: -LER

The plural ending in Turkish is **-ler** or **-lar**. If the last vowel in the base (the main part of the word) is a front vowel – **e, i, ö** or **ü** – then the plural suffix is **-ler**:

ev house	**evler** houses
kedi cat	**kediler** cats
göz eye	**gözler** eyes
gül rose	**güller** roses

If the last vowel in the base is a back vowel – **a, ı, o** or **u**, then the plural suffix is **-lar**:

kova bucket	**kovalar** buckets
balık fish	**balıklar** fish (*plural*)
sabun soap	**sabunlar** soaps

Almost all concrete nouns in Turkish have plurals. Examples:

para money	**paralar** money(s)
toz dust	**tozlar** dust(s)

However, when numbers are used, the noun is *always* in the singular:

iki oda two rooms
on gün ten days
dört büyük otel four large hotels

When an adjective takes the plural suffix, it means that the adjective is being used as a noun:

Kısalar güzel değil. The short ones are not nice.

Yaşlılar evde. The old ones (the old folks) are at home.
Küçükler bahçede. The little ones (the children) are in the garden.

Vocabulary

doktor	doctor
mühendis	engineer
avukat	lawyer
polis	police, policeman
kapı	door
pencere	window
duvar	wall
oda	room
ev	house
adam	man
kadın	woman, female
erkek	male person
kız	girl
oğlan	boy
genç	young
yaşlı } **ihtiyar** }	old (in age)
eski	old
yeni	new
renk	colour
beyaz	white
siyah	black
sarı	yellow
mavi	blue
yeşil	green
iyi	good
kötü } **fena** }	bad
ucuz	cheap
pahalı	expensive
güzel	beautiful, nice
çirkin	ugly
zengin	rich
fakir	poor
sıcak	hot
soğuk	cold

çalışkan	hard-working
tembel	lazy
Türk	Turkish (person)
İngiliz	English (person)
yorgun	tired
çocuk	child
gün	day
sabah	morning
akşam	evening
hava	weather

12 Personal suffixes

These suffixes show the person and number of the subject, and have the function of the verb 'to be' in English. They are used where in English you would say '*I am* well', '*He is* a doctor', etc. The set below indicates present time.

-(Y)İM	I am
-SİN	you are (singular, informal)
-DİR	he/she/it is
-(Y)İZ	we are
-SİNİZ	you are (plural/formal singular)
-DİRLER	they are

(Parts of the suffixes are enclosed above in brackets: this means that under certain conditions these parts are not used.)

-(Y)İM: I am

In Turkish, two vowels do not come together in the word (except in some words of non-Turkish origin). So when the base of a word ends in a vowel and the suffix also begins with a vowel, a buffer is needed between these two vowels. With most suffixes, this buffer is **-y-**.

The vowel in this suffix has four possible ways of harmonising: it can be **i, ı, ü** or **u**, depending on the previous vowel. There are thus eight possibilities – variants – for the suffix **-(Y)İM**, depending on whether the **-y-** buffer is needed:

After bases ending in vowels, the variants are **-yim, -yım, -yüm, -yum**. Examples:

yaşlıyım	I am old
iyiyim	I am well
kötüyüm	I am bad/unwell
mutluyum	I am happy

After bases ending in consonants, the variants are **-im, -ım, -üm, -um**. Examples:

İngilizim	I am British
çalışkanım	I am hard-working
Türküm	I am Turkish
doktorum	I am a doctor

-SİN: *you are (singular, informal)*

This second person singular suffix is used when addressing people with whom one is on informal terms. Its variants are **-sin, -sın, -sün, -sun**. Examples:

gençsin	you are young
yaşlısın	you are old
kötüsün	you are bad
doktorsun	you are a doctor

-DİR: *he/she/it is*

In colloquial speech, this ending is usually omitted:

genç	he is young
sıcak	it is hot

The gender of the subject is understood from the context. But the suffix is used when the speaker wants to emphasise something or make a generalisation that is valid for all cases.

Doktordur. He *is* a doctor.
Gelen polistir. It must be the police who came.
Pırlanta pahalıdır. Diamonds are expensive.

The suffix indicates shades of meaning which become clear if the whole context is known. It has eight variants: **-dir, -dır, -dür, -dur** and **-tir, -tır, -tür, -tur**. Examples:

mühendistir he is an engineer	**yeşildir** it is green
sıcaktır it is hot	**sarıdır** it is yellow
soğuktur it is cold	**kötüdür** it is bad
Türktür she is Turkish	**uzundur** she is tall

(handwritten note: ↙ sounds like "e")

The **-DİR** suffix can also be added to other personal suffixes, to indicate an assumption, a certainty, about that person on the part of the speaker:

Hastasındır. You must be ill.
Akıllıyımdır: I certainly am clever.

-(Y)İZ: we are

The variants are:

after vowels **-yiz, -yız, -yüz, -yuz**
after consonants **-iz, -ız, -üz, -uz**

iyiyiz we are well	**İngiliziz** we are British
hastayız we are ill	**kadınız** we are women
üzgünüz we are sad	**Türküz** we are Turkish
mutluyuz we are happy	**doktoruz** we are doctors

-SİNİZ: you are (plural and formal singular)

The variants are **-siniz, -sınız, -sünüz, -sunuz**

zenginsiniz	you are rich
fakirsiniz	you are poor
yorgunsunuz	you are tired
Türksünüz	you are Turkish

-DİRLER: they are

The variants are

(handwritten note: lar / ler)

-tirler, -tırlar, -türler, -turlar and **-dirler, -dırlar, -dürler, -durlar**

iyidirler	they are well
yorgundurlar	they are tired
büyüktürler	they are big
çalışkandırlar	they are hard-working

It is also possible to omit **-dir** and just have **-ler** to indicate the plural person, if there is no separate word for the subject:

iyiler they are well
yorgunlar they are tired

When the subject has the plural suffix, the **-LER** part of this ending (or often the whole of it) is usually omitted:

Odalar küçüktür. The rooms are small.
Oteller pahalı. Hotels are expensive.
Adamlar yaşlı. The men are old.
Çocuklar tembeldir. The children are lazy.

13 Personal pronouns

ben	I	**biz**	we
sen	you (sing. informal)	**siz**	you (plural and formal singular)
o	he/she/it	**onlar**	they

There is no distinction between 'he', 'she' and 'it' in Turkish. The context gives the clue to the gender of the person involved.

Sen is the singular, informal 'you', rather like the French *tu* or the German *du*. **Sen** is used when speaking to close friends, family and children. **Siz** is used for acquaintances, people with whom you have only a formal relationship. In rural areas, however, this distinction breaks down, and **sen** is used for anyone. If you are worried about giving offence, keep to **siz**, but do not be put out if you are addressed as **sen**.

As the personal suffixes give the person and number of the subject, personal pronouns are generally not used as the subject of a sentence in colloquial speech. They are used to put special emphasis on the person, or to make comparisons or contrasts between people. Examples:

Siz gençsiniz, ben yaşlıyım. You are young, I am old.
Biz Türküz, onlar İngiliz. We are Turkish, they are British.

In colloquial speech, the plural suffix **-LER** is sometimes added to the plural pronouns **biz** and **siz**, giving us **bizler** and **sizler**. The meaning is not affected by this addition.

14 Demonstratives

There are three demonstratives in Turkish: **bu** 'this', **şu** 'that/this', **o** 'that'. They can be either adjectives (qualifying a noun) or pronouns (standing in place of a noun) and are used like the English demonstratives, but **şu** has certain features peculiar to it.

a) The use of **şu** is usually accompanied by a gesture towards the thing referred to, which should be so located that it is possible to make such a gesture.

b) It is also used to refer to something which is going to be mentioned; in this use **şu** can be translated as 'the following':

Şu renkler güzel: mavi, yeşil, sarı.
These (The following) colours are nice: blue, green, yellow.

Bu soğuk. This is cold.
O küçük. That is small.
Şu ucuz. That is cheap.

Like adjectives, the demonstratives can precede nouns:

Bu oda büyük. This room is big.
O çocuk kız. That child is (a) girl.
Şu duvar beyaz, şu duvar sarı. That wall is white, that wall is yellow.

If there is an adjective before the noun, the demonstrative precedes the adjective:

Bu kırmızı palto güzel. This red coat is nice.
Şu yaşlı adam hasta. That old man is ill.

Unlike English, if the noun is plural, the demonstrative, when used as an adjective, stays in the singular:

O arabalar pahalı. Those (lit. that) cars are expensive.

As pronouns, however, the demonstratives can take the plural ending, and **n** is then added to the base: **bunlar** 'these', **şunlar** 'those/these', **onlar** 'those'. Again, **n** is added to the base whenever demonstratives take a suffix.

Exercise 4

Translate the following into English:
1 kısa saç

27

2 genç bir avukat
3 kırmızı bir palto
4 mavi gözler
5 büyük oteller
6 küçük evler
7 Ben Türküm, siz İngilizsiniz.
8 Kadın hasta.
9 Tembelsin.
10 Küçük çocuklar yorgun.

15 Negatives: non-verbal

In sentences where there is no full verb, but one of the different forms
of 'to be' is used (see section 12), the negative is formed with the word
değil 'not'. Personal suffixes are attached to **değil**.

Hasta değilim. I am not ill.
Türk değilsiniz. You are not Turkish.
Oda büyük değil. The room is not big.
Deniz sıcak değil. The sea is not warm (lit. hot).
Yorgun değiliz. We are not tired.

16 Yes/No questions

The question marker **Mİ** is used to make questions which require yes/no
answers. In non-verbal sentences **Mİ** comes before the personal suffixes.
It has the variants **mi, mı, mü, mu**. In writing, the question marker is
separated from the previous part of the word by a space, but it still
harmonises with the preceding vowel.

Güzel miyim? Am I nice?
Yorgun musun? Are you tired?
Oda temiz mi? Is the room clean?
Otel pahalı mıdır? Is the hotel expensive?
Çalışkan mıyız? Are we hard-working?
İyi misiniz? Are you well?
Ucuzlar mı? Are they cheap?
Evler ucuz mu? Are the houses cheap?

28

The answers to these questions can be:

Yes, _____ + person: Evet, _____ + $\begin{cases} \text{-(Y)İM} & \text{-(Y)İZ} \\ \text{-SİN} & \text{-SİNİZ} \\ \text{-DİR} & \text{-DİRLER} \end{cases}$

or

No, _____ + **değil** + person   **Hayır,** _____ + **değil** + person

Hava soğuk mu?   **Hayır, soğuk değil.**
Is the weather cold?   No, it is not cold.
İyi misiniz?   **Evet, iyiyiz.**
Are you well?   Yes, we are well.   *mu, etc*

The question marker is quite mobile in the sentence, and always follows the word which is being questioned:

Yaşlı doktor Türk mü? Is the old doctor *Turkish*?
Yaşlı doktor mu Türk? Is it the *old doctor* who is Turkish?

The question marker is not used if there is an interrogative (a question word like 'what', 'why', 'who' etc.) in the sentence (see section 18).

When the question involves a choice, then the question marker **Mİ** is used twice:

Deniz sıcak mı soğuk mu? Is the sea hot or cold?
Otel ucuz mu pahalı mı? Is the hotel cheap or expensive?
Ev büyük mü küçük mü? Is the house big or small?

Mİ is also used with **değil** in questions like:

Yorgun musun, değil misin? Are you tired or not?
Sarı mı, değil mi? Is it yellow or not?

17 Non-verbal negative questions

The sequence here is:

base   +   negative   +   question   +   person
Yorgun   **değil**   **mi**   **yim**
Yorgun değil miyim? Am I not tired?

Zengin değil misiniz? Are you not rich?
Ucuz değil mi(dir)? Isn't it cheap?

But note the third person plural (with the third person plural, the personal suffix comes before the question marker):

Zengin değiller mi? Aren't they rich?
Adamlar zengin değil(ler) mi? Aren't the men rich?

18 Interrogatives: kim, ne, nasıl ('who', 'what', 'how')

kim means 'who' – plural **kimler**

Kim yorgun(dur)? Who is tired?
Kim doktor? Who is (a) doctor?
Kimler İngiliz? Who is (Which people are) British?
Kimler Türk? Who is (Which people are) Turkish?

In the questions above, **kim** 'who' is the subject. These are non-verbal sentences; the third person singular form of 'to be' **-DİR** occupies the position of a verb. However, as we explained in section 12, this suffix is generally omitted, so the absence of a personal suffix here indicates the third person: 'is' in English. Except when we make changes for reasons of style, a Turkish sentence normally begins with the subject and ends with the verb (or what stands for a verb) and the personal suffix indicating the subject is added to this. So the question **Kim yorgun(dur)?** is translated literally 'Who tired is?'(Who is tired?) and **Kim doktor?** lit. 'Who doctor is?' (Who is (a) doctor?).

If we change the order of these words in the question we have: **Yorgun kim?** lit. 'Tired who is?' **Yorgun** is now the subject, meaning 'the *one* who is tired', and the question now translates 'The one who is tired (he) is who?' In normal English it is 'Who is tired?' As you see, the two questions **Kim yorgun?** and **Yorgun kim?** are translated in the same way: the word order makes them function differently, but the essential meaning is not very different.

In answering such questions you just replace the interrogative (the question word) with the answer word – or words:
Kim doktor?   Ahmet doktor.
Ahmet is a doctor. (**Ahmet:** male first name)
Kim yorgun?   Ayşe yorgun.
Ayşe is tired. (**Ayşe:** female first name)

When an interrogative like **kim** is not the subject of the sentence it can take the personal suffixes:

Ben kimim? Who am I? (the subject is **ben** 'I')
Kimsiniz? Who are you? (the subject is **siz** 'you' – omitted)
Nesiniz? What are you? (the subject is **siz** 'you' – omitted)
Nasılım? How am I? (How do I look?) (the subject is **ben** 'I' – omitted)

ne means 'what' – plural **neler**

Ne kırmızı? What is red?
Answer: **Halı kırmızı.** The carpet is red.
Kırmızı ne? Red is what?
Answer: **Kırmızı bir renk.** Red is a colour.
Ben neyim? What am I?
Answer: **Siz İngilizsiniz.** You are British.
       Siz doktorsunuz. You are a doctor.

nasıl means 'how', "what sort of" (and, more basic meaning)

Nasılsınız?/Siz nasılsınız? How are you? (remember that the personal pronoun is not necessary unless there is special emphasis on it)
Çocuklar nasıl? How are the children?
Hava nasıl? How is the weather? (i.e. What is the weather like?)
Nasıl hava? What sort of weather?

The question marker **Mİ** is not used when there is an interrogative in the same sentence. The only exception is when a question is quoted and then put to someone as a question, for example:

Hava nasıl mı? How is the weather, is this the question?
Ben neyim mi? What am I, is this the question (is this what is asked)?

19 'and', 'but', 'or'

ve means 'and'

Otel temiz ve ucuz(dur). The hotel is clean and cheap.
Zengin adam yaşlı ve hasta. The rich man is old and ill.
Uzun ve kırmızı palto güzel. The long (and) red coat is nice.
Halı yeşil, sarı ve mavi(dir). The carpet is green, yellow and blue.
yeşil, sarı ve mavi halı the green, yellow and blue carpet

In Turkish there are three words for 'but', all currently used: **ama, fakat, ancak**. This is not unusual in Turkish, where we have a large number of words taken from Arabic and Persian used side by side with words which are Turkish in origin.

Halı güzel fakat pahalı.
Halı güzel ama pahalı. } The carpet is nice but expensive.
Halı güzel ancak pahalı.

Ancak also has another meaning, 'just', 'only':

ancak 'but' **Yorgunum, ancak mutluyum.**
I am tired but happy.
ancak 'just, only' **Ancak bir küçük halı alabildik.**
We managed to buy only one small carpet.

There are several words for 'or' in Turkish: **veya, ya da, yahut, yahut ta**. All are currently used; which to use is mostly a matter of personal preference and style, but **veya** and **ya da** enjoy greater popularity now and are also the preferred forms in formal written Turkish.

Öğretmen veya öğrenci değil, doktor.
He is not a teacher or a student, he is a doctor.

CONVERSATION

- Günaydın.
- Günaydın.
- Nasılsınız?
- İyiyim, teşekkür ederim. Siz nasılsınız?
- Ben de iyiyim, teşekkür ederim.
- Bu sabah deniz çok güzel.
- Evet, ama soğuk değil mi?
- Hayır, soğuk değil, ama hava soğuk.
- Evet. İyi günler.
- İyi günler.

Note: Ben de iyiyim 'I too am well': **de**, which means 'too', 'also', harmonises with the base – variants are **de, da** – but it is always written separately. It can also be used to mean 'and', 'as well'.
Adam da yorgun(dur). The man too/also is tired. (various people are tired, so is the man)

Adam yorgun(dur) da. The man is tired as well. (as well as being various other things he is also tired)
Oda büyük, güzel de. The room is big, and it is nice. (it is also nice)

Exercise 5

A Translate into English:
1 Genç kadın yorgun değil.
2 Büyük otel ucuz mu?
3 Hava nasıl, soğuk mu?
4 Adam kim?
5 Halı mavi mi, yeşil mi?
6 Siyah araba yeni değil mi?
7 Kapı kapalı ama pencere açık.

B Translate into Turkish:
1 The young man is not a policeman.
2 What colour is the house?
3 The blue and red carpet is big and beautiful, but it is expensive too.
4 Isn't the room small?
5 How are you?
6 How is the old man, is he well?
7 Green and yellow colours are nice.

Lesson 3

20 -DE: locational suffix (locative case)

This suffix indicates where an action takes place or where a person or thing is located. It means 'in', 'on', 'at'. It has four variants: **-de, -da** and **-te, -ta** (see section 6):

evde at home　　　　　　　　**işte** at work
sinemada in the cinema　　　**masada** on the table
Kırmızı örtü masada. The red cloth is on the table.
Çocuklar okulda mı? Are the children at school?
Yaşlı kadın evde değil. The old woman is not at home.

Personal pronouns and demonstratives can also take this suffix:

bende on me, in me　　　　　**bunda** in this, on this
sende on you, in you　　　　　**onda** in that, on that

21 var: there is/there are

Var means 'there is', 'there are', and 'there exists'. It is mostly used with the third person, but can also take all the other personal endings.

Sokakta arabalar var. There are cars in the street.
Odada iki pencere ve bir kapı var. There are two windows and one door in the room.

With first and second person suffixes, the sense conveyed is that of being included in something.

Toplantıda varım. I am included in the meeting.
Yemekte varsınız. You are included in the dinner (meal)/You are going to be present at dinner (meal).

22 yok: there isn't/there aren't

Yok shows the absence of something, that it does not exist.

Sokakta araba yok. There are no cars in the street. (lit. is no car)

Ankara'da deniz yok. There is no sea in Ankara. (after the proper noun **Ankara** an apostrophe separates the suffix, but harmony continues as usual).

Televizyonda iyi bir film yok. There isn't a good film on TV.

Bu akşam evde yokuz. We are not at home this evening.

Yok is also used to mean 'no':

Hasta mısın? Yok.   Are you ill? No.

As **yok** acts as a negative for **var**, **değil** is not normally used with **var**. In very limited contexts **değil** can be used with either **var** or **yok** to mean roughly 'it is not that ...', for example:

Çok iş var değil, ama ben yorgunum. It isn't that there is much work, but I am tired.

Para yok değil, ama az. It isn't that there isn't any money, but there's not much (lit. it is little).

23 Questions with var and yok

The question marker **Mİ** is placed after **var** and **yok** to form questions.

Sokakta kırmızı bir araba var mı? Is there a red car in the street?

Okulda öğrenci var mı? Are there students in the school?

Evde üç oda yok mu? Aren't there three rooms in the house?

Sende para var mı? Is there any money on you?

Hayır, bende para yok, sende de yok mu? No, there isn't (any) on me, isn't there (any) on you either (lit. too)?

With interrogatives:

Telefonda kim var? Who is on the phone?

Sokakta ne var? What's in the street?

Yemekte ne var? What's for lunch/dinner (lit. at the meal)?

24 Numerals: cardinal

sıfır	zero	**üç**	three
bir	one	**dört**	four
iki	two	**beş**	five

altı	six	elli	fifty
yedi	seven	altmış	sixty
sekiz	eight	yetmiş	seventy
dokuz	nine	seksen	eighty
on	ten	doksan	ninety
on bir	eleven	yüz	hundred
on sekiz	eighteen	bin	thousand
yirmi	twenty	milyon	million
otuz	thirty	milyar	billion (1000 million)
kırk	forty		

yüz elli (a) hundred and fifty
iki yüz seksen yedi two hundred and eighty-seven
bin altı yüz kırk iki 1642
yirmi bin beş yüz 20500

Where there is a compound number Turkish does not have 'and' between the component numbers. And remember, when there is a number the following noun is always in the singular.

yarım means 'half', 'half a ...':
yarım kilo elma half a kilo of apples
yarım fincan kahve half a cup of coffee
yarım saat half an hour

buçuk means '... and a half' and follows a number:
bir buçuk kilo elma one and a half kilos of apples
bir buçuk fincan kahve one and a half cups of coffee
bir buçuk saat an hour and a half
beş buçuk gün five and a half days

çeyrek means 'a quarter'; it is mostly used for talking about time:
çeyrek saat a quarter of an hour
bir saat bir çeyrek an hour and a quarter

Fractions are usually expressed as 'number + **de** + number':
dörtte bir one in four (one fourth)
onda iki two in ten (two tenths)
üçte iki two in three (two thirds)
yüzde on ten percent (the percentage sign precedes the numeral: %90)
Servis ücreti yüzde onbeştir. Service charge is fifteen percent.

Vocabulary

masa   table

iskemle } sandalye }	chair
tavan	ceiling
yer	floor, seat, ground, place
lamba	lamp
dolap	cupboard
koltuk	armchair
fincan	cup
tepsi	tray
arkadaş	friend
misafir	guest
insan	person, human being
hayvan	animal
resim	picture
kalem	pen/pencil
kitap	book
defter	notebook
çanta	bag
perde	curtain
pembe	pink
kahverengi	brown
yol	way, path
metro	underground train
akıllı	clever
aptal	stupid
geç erken	late early } (used for things and time)
aç	hungry
tok	full
dar	narrow
geniş	wide
ağır	heavy
hafif	light
ince	slim, thin
kalın	thick
saat	clock, watch, time, hour
yastık	cushion
cadde	road, avenue (a main road)
bahçe	garden

Exercise 6

A Translate into English:
1 Bu odada iki pencere, bir kapı, bir büyük masa, beş iskemle ve bir koltuk var.
2 Kahverengi koltukta iki yeşil yastık var.
3 Yerde ne renk halı var?
4 Bahçede kim var?
5 Odada dolap yok mu?
6 Pencerede perde yok.
7 Evde misafir var.

B Translate into Turkish:
1 There are books, pens and notebooks on the table.
2 There is no money on me.
3 There aren't (any) animals in the small garden.
4 Isn't there a car in the street?
5 In the room, what colour are the walls and the curtains?
6 What is in the heavy box?
7 Is there a good film at the cinema?

25 çok, bir çok, bir kaç, hiç

Çok is a word you will hear a lot. Before adjectives it translates as 'very', before nouns as 'many, much, a lot'.

Çok güzel. Very nice.
Çok iyiyim. I am very well.

Bir çok means 'very many, a lot of, a number of'.

Bu kitapta bir çok resim var. There are many pictures in this book.

Bir kaç means 'several' and also 'a few'.

Kutuda bir kaç kalem var. There are a few pens in the box.
Bir kaç saat bekledik. We waited several hours.

Hiç means several things depending on the context.

It can mean 'any', 'any ... at all':
Sende hiç para var mı? Have you any money at all?

('Any' is often omitted when translating into Turkish: 'Have you any money?' is **Paran var mı?** But when there is a meaning conveying 'at all', then **hiç** is used: **Hiç paran var mı?** Have you any money at all?)

With negatives **hiç** means 'none', 'none at all', 'not at all':
Hiç güzel değil. It is not nice at all.
Hiç yok. There is none/There is none at all.

26 Measurements

gram gramme
kilo kilo
iki yüz gram peynir two hundred grammes of cheese

Remember, with numbers the noun is used in the singular in Turkish:
iki kilo et two kilos of meat

metre metre
santimetre or **santim** centimetre
kilometre kilometre
mil mile (nautical mile)
Plaj iki kilometre uzakta. The beach is two kilometres away.

litre litre
on litre benzin ten litres of petrol

27 Interrogatives: kimde, nerede, kaç ('on whom', 'where', 'how many')

Kimde means 'on whom' (**kim** 'who' + **de** 'on', 'at', 'in').

Kimde beş yüz lira var? (lit. On whom is there 500 lira?) Who has got 500 lira?
Kitap kimde? (lit. On whom is the book?) Who has got the book?

Nerede means 'where', or more specifically 'at where', 'in where', 'on where (i.e. on what)'. It is formed with **nere** (location) + **de**.

Kitap nerede? Where is the book?
Masada. (It's) on the table.

Araba nerede? Where is the car?
Sokakta. In the street.

Kaç means 'how many?' or 'how much?' The answer to questions with **kaç** always includes a number or a word indicating an amount.

Bu okulda kaç öğrenci var? How many students are there in this school?
Çok öğrenci var. There are many students.
Bu palto kaç lira? How much is this coat? (lit. How many lira is this coat?)
Seksen bin lira. It's eighty thousand lira.

CONVERSATION

- Günaydın. Buyurun efendim.
- Günaydın. Üzüm var mı?
- Var efendim.
- Bir kilo lütfen.
- Peki.
- Kaç lira?
- Bir kilo sekiz yüz elli lira.
- Buyurun, teşekkür ederim.
- İyi günler.
- İyi günler.

28 -Lİ: 'with', 'having', 'containing'

The suffix **-Lİ** is used to indicate that something has a certain quality or contains something. It is added to nouns to form adjectives. It has four variants: **-li, -lı, -lü, -lu**.

süt milk   **sütlü** with milk, milky
Bir sütlü kahve lütfen. A coffee with milk please.

şeker sugar	**şekerli** with sugar, containing sugar
hız speed	**hızlı** speedy
kuvvet } strength	**kuvvetli** } strong
güç	**güçlü**
yağmur rain	**yağmurlu** rainy
para money	**paralı** with money; rich

40

Giriş paralıdır. Entry is with money (with a fee: i.e. you pay to enter).
paralı bir adam a rich man
banyo bath   **banyolu** with a bath
banyolu oda room with bath
beş odalı bir ev a five-roomed house
şapkalı kadın woman with a hat
kırmızı paltolu çocuk child in a red coat (lit. red-coated child)

 Used with colours it means 'in those colours', for example:

sarılı kadın woman in yellow
kırmızılı, yeşilli bir elbise a dress in red and green
renkli multi-coloured

Similarly with flavours:

lezzetli delicious, tasty (of food)   **lezzet** taste (of food)
tuzlu salty
biberli peppery

 With the interrogative **ne, neli** means 'with what flavour?':

Dondurma neli? What flavour ice-cream?
Çikolatalı ve çilekli. Chocolate and strawberry flavours.

The suffix **-Lİ** is also used with place names to indicate a person from that area:

İstanbullu person from Istanbul
Londralı Londoner
Üsküdarlı person from Üsküdar, a district of Istanbul
köylü villager
şehirli }
kentli } city/town dweller

With names of countries it refers to citizens of those countries:

Amerikalı an American   **Mısırlı** an Egyptian

but we do not say **İngiltereli** or **Türkiyeli,** because some countries have special terms for denoting citizens; for instance, an Englishman is **İngiliz,** a Turk is **Türk,** a German is **Alman.** (See section 136.)

29 -SİZ: 'without', 'not having', 'not containing'

-SİZ is added to nouns to form adjectives meaning 'without'. Variants are **-siz, -sız, -süz, -suz.**

sütsüz without milk
şekersiz without sugar
kuvvetsiz without any strength, weak
banyosuz without a bath
yağmursuz without rain
renksiz colourless
lezzetsiz bland, without taste
parasız without money, poor; free
Müzeye giriş parasızdır. Entry to the museum is free.
İçkiler parasız. The drinks are free.

Exercise 7

A Translate into English:
1 Bugün hava soğuk değil, fakat yağmurlu.
2 Banyolu iki oda lütfen.
3 Çikolatalı dondurma var mı?
4 Bu ev kaç odalı?
5 Sokakta mavi paltolu üç çocuk var.

B Translate into Turkish:
1 A coffee with milk please.
2 I am not from Ankara, I am a Londoner.
3 Where is the book with pictures?
4 How much is a room with bath?
5 The blue carpet is small but expensive.

Lesson 4

30 Verbs

Verbs are generally given with a **-mek** or **-mak** suffix. This is how you find verbs in most dictionaries, and this form is called the infinitive. The suffix is left out when a verb is used in a sentence, except when you want to use the infinitive form; for example, **gelmek** means 'to come', **gel-** is the base 'come', and **-mek** is the infinitive suffix 'to'. All the suffixes that a verb can take are added to the base after removing the **-mek** or **-mak** suffix.

31 The past tense

The past tense is used to express things done and actions completed in the past. It translates the English forms 'I have seen', 'I did see' and 'I saw'.

The **-Dİ** suffix is used to form the past in the following way:

a) The infinitive **-mek, -mak** is removed and **-Dİ** is added to the base; **gelmek** 'to come', **gel** 'come', **gel + Dİ = geldi** 'came'.

b) Personal suffixes, that is endings which indicate the person doing the action, are placed after the past suffix **-Dİ**.

Here are some examples:

yemek	to eat	**yedi**	ate
içmek	to drink	**içti**	drank
asmak	to hang	**astı**	hung
kalmak	to stay	**kaldı**	stayed
görmek	to see	**gördü**	saw
örtmek	to cover	**örttü**	covered
koymak	to put	**koydu**	put
koşmak	to run	**koştu**	ran

The past tense suffix has eight variants:
-di, -dı, -dü, -du,
-ti, -tı, -tü, -tu.

(For the harmony rules that bring about these changes, look back at section 5.)

Personal suffixes that are added to the past tense suffix **-Dİ** to indicate the subject of the verb are as follows:

-M   I
-N   you (familiar, singular)
—   he, she, it
-K   we
-NİZ   you (plural or formal); variants **-niz, -nız, -nüz, -nuz**
(-LER)   they; variants **-ler, -lar**

There is no personal suffix for the third person.

The order of the suffixes is as follows:
verb + past + person
oku   **du**   **m**   **okudum** I read

geldim	I came	**baktım**	I looked
geldin	you came	**baktın**	you looked
geldi	he/she/it came	**baktı**	he/she/it looked
geldik	we came	**baktık**	we looked
geldiniz	you came	**baktınız**	you looked
geldiler	they came	**baktılar**	they looked
gördüm	I saw	**koştum**	I ran
gördün	you saw	**koştun**	you ran
gördü	he/she/it saw	**koştu**	he/she/it ran
gördük	we saw	**koştuk**	we ran
gördünüz	you saw	**koştunuz**	you ran
gördüler	they saw	**koştular**	they ran

As discussed in lesson 2, you do not need to use a subject pronoun like **ben, sen** etc.: the subject is contained in the verb.

Güzel bir otelde kaldım. I stayed at a nice hotel.
Çok yemek yedi. He ate a lot of food.
Bir bardak su içtin. You drank a glass of water.
Televizyonda güzel bir film gördük. We saw a good film on television.
Plajda oturdular, konuştular. They sat and talked on the beach.
Çok kitap aldınız. You bought a lot of books.

44

Only when you want to give special emphasis or contrast persons do you use a subject pronoun:

Ben güzel bir otelde kaldım. *I* stayed at a nice hotel. (not you, not him, but *I*)

Vocabulary

yazmak	to write	**yemek**	to eat
okumak	to read	**içmek**	to drink
başlamak	to begin, to start	**almak**	to take, get, buy
çalışmak	to work, study	**vermek**	to give
anlamak	to understand	**bitirmek**	to finish (something)
oturmak	to sit, reside	**bitmek**	to come to an end
yüzmek	to swim	**uyumak**	to sleep
açmak	to open, turn on	**binmek**	to get on
kapamak	to close, turn off	**inmek**	to get off
kalmak	to stay	**görmek**	to see
gitmek	to go	**dün**	yesterday

Exercise 8

A   Translate into English:
1   İstanbul'da on beş gün kaldım.
2   İki saat çalıştım.
3   Bodrum'da denizde yüzdüm, plajda oturdum.
4   Güzel bir yemek yedik ve şarap içtik.
5   Odada oturdum ve mektup yazdım.

B   Translate into Turkish:
1   I read two books.
2   He worked.
3   Yesterday we swam a lot.
4   The child stayed at home.
5   You (pl.) understood.

32 Negative with -Dİ

The suffix **-ME** is added to verbs to form the negative. When you want to say that a given action has not been done, you put the **-ME** negative suffix after the verb base. It has two different forms, **-me** and **-ma,** and is followed by the past and personal suffixes:

verb + negative + past + person
gel   **me**   **di**   **m**   **gelmedim** I did not come

okumadım	I did not read
gelmedin	you did not come
görmedi	he did not see
anlamadık	we did not understand
açmadınız	you did not open
yüzmediler	they did not swim

Exercise 9

Translate into Turkish:
1 I did not stay in a hotel.
2 He did not understand.
3 It did not begin.
4 You (pl.) did not see.
5 They did not sit on the beach.

33 Questions with -Dİ

In questions in the past tense which require a yes or no answer, the question marker **Mİ** is placed *after* all the suffixes, and it harmonises like all the other suffixes (see section 5) although it is written separately.

verb + past + person + **Mİ** (question)

gel	**di**	**k**	**mi?**	**geldik mi?** have we arrived?
yüz	**dü**	**nüz**	**mü?**	**yüzdünüz mü?** did you swim?
oku	**du**	**lar**	**mı?**	**okudular mı?** did they read?
bak	**tı**	**—**	**mı?**	**baktı mı?** did he look?

If the question is in the negative, the negative suffix is placed *before* all the other suffixes:

```
verb + negative + past + person + Mİ
gel    me        di     k         mi    gelmedik mi? did we not
                                         come?
```

yüzmediniz mi? did you not swim?
okumadınız mı? did you not read?
bakmadılar mı? did they not look?

When you want to question some other point in the sentence, rather than simply asking whether an action has or has not been done, **Mİ** is placed after the point you wish to question:

Ali dün İstanbul'a gitti. Yesterday Ali went to Istanbul.
Ali dün İstanbul'a gitti mi? Did Ali *go* to Istanbul yesterday?
Ali dün İstanbul'a mı gitti? Did Ali go to *Istanbul* yesterday?
Ali dün mü İstanbul'a gitti? Did Ali go to Istanbul *yesterday?*
Ali mi dün İstanbul'a gitti? Did *Ali* go to Istanbul yesterday?

When a question word like 'who' or 'what' is used, the question marker **Mİ** is not used:

Kim geldi? Who came?
Dün akşam nerede yediniz? Where did you eat last night?
Adam kaç lira verdi? How many lira (i.e. how much money) did the man give?

Exercise 10

Answer the following questions both in the affirmative and in the negative:
Example: **İstanbul'da kaldın mı?**
   Evet, İstanbul'da kaldım./Hayır, İstanbul'da kalmadım.

1 Elma yediniz mi?
2 Otelde çay içtiniz mi (pl.)?
3 Gazete aldın mı?
4 Sinemada uyudum mu?
5 Çok çalıştık mı?

34 -(Y)İ: definite object (accusative case)

This suffix translates in English as the definite article 'the', but it is used *only* when a specific, definite thing or person is the object of the verb. A person or thing is specific or definite if it is described in some detail, or if there has been a reference to it previously. So if the object of the verb is of this kind, it must take the -(Y)İ suffix, but if the object is non-specific, then this suffix is not used. For example, in the sentence 'I bought a coat', 'I' is the subject (the person who has done the action of buying), and 'a coat' is the object (the thing that has been affected by the action of buying) and it is non-specific: 'a' coat. The Turkish translation is:

Bir palto aldım. I bought a (or one) coat.
or
Palto aldım. I bought (a) coat.
(in a broad sense it could also be coat<u>s</u>, although there is no plural marker)

In the sentence 'I bought the coat', by using the definite article 'the' you have specified the coat: it is not any coat, but that particular one (perhaps the one that was mentioned to you). As the object is definite, in Turkish it must take the -(Y)İ suffix:

Paltoyu aldım. I bought the coat.

Gazete okudu. He read (a) newspaper.
Gazeteyi okudu. He read the newspaper.

Yemek yedik. We ate food (a meal).
Yemeği yedik. We ate the food (the meal).

Two vowels do not come together in Turkish. When a suffix is essentially a vowel, a buffer is needed between that vowel and the final vowel of the base. This buffer is usually **-y-: kapı – kapıyı, oda – odayı, örtü – örtüyü**, etc. The suffix -(Y)İ therefore has eight variants: **-i, -ı, -ü, -u** after consonants and **-yi, -yı, -yü, -yu** after vowels.

Proper nouns, because they are always specific, will always take the -(Y)İ suffix if they are in the object position:
Ali'yi gördüm. I saw Ali.
Ankara'yı beğendim. I liked Ankara.

48

Similarly, if the object is a pronoun, it must take the definite object suffix **-(Y)İ**:

beni	me	**bizi**	us
seni	you	**sizi**	you
onu	him, her, it	**onları**	them

Seni sinemada gördüm. I saw you in the cinema.
Bizi beklediniz mi? Did you wait for us?

The definite object forms of **bu**, **şu** and **o** are **bunu**, **şunu** and **onu**:

Onu içtin mi? Did you drink it?
Bunu okumadım. I did not read this.
Şunu açmadılar. They did not open that.

35 Interrogatives: kimi, neyi, nereyi, ne zaman

The interrogatives **kim** 'who', **ne** 'what' and **nere** 'where' take the definite object case ending when they are the direct object of a verb:

kimi whom
Sokakta kimi gördün? Whom did you see in the street?

neyi what
Neyi okudun? What (specific, definite thing) did you read?
Neyi okudun, kitabı mı, gazeteyi mi? What did you read, the book or the newspaper? (indefinite: **Ne okudun, kitap mı, gazete mi?** What did you read, a book or a newspaper?).

nereyi which place, what place
İstanbul'da nereyi gördünüz? Which place did you see in Istanbul?

ne zaman when
Ali ne zaman gitti? When did Ali go?
Kitabı ne zaman okudunuz? When did you read the book?
Ne zaman çalıştık? When did we work?

Vocabulary

meyve	fruit	**durak**	bus stop
sebze	vegetable	**havlu**	towel
çiçek	flower	**su**	water
istasyon	station	**sabun**	soap

sigara	cigarette	yatmak	to lie down, go to bed
sigara içmek	to smoke	kalkmak	to get up; to depart
bırakmak	to leave		(of planes, trains
dolap	cupboard		etc)
radyo	radio	aramak	to look for
televizyon	TV	yapmak	to do
postane	post office	getirmek	to bring (along)
eczane	chemist	götürmek	to take (away, along)
hastane	hospital	bilmek	to know
girmek	to go in, enter	konuşmak	to speak
göstermek	to show, point out	anlamak	to understand
çıkmak	to come out	göstermek	to show, point out
dinlemek	to listen	satmak	to sell
duymak	to hear	geçmek	to pass, cross
bakmak	to look	istemek	to want

Exercise 11

A Translate into English:
1 Dolabı açtım ve büyük çantayı aldım.
2 Bunu kim yaptı?
3 Masayı görmedim.
4 Hava çok kötü, uçaklar kalkmadı.
5 Radyoyu açtım, televizyonu kapadım.

B Translate into Turkish:
1 I left the car in the street.
2 Did you eat the apple?
3 I did not show him the post office.
4 I did not see London.
5 Did you (pl.) understand this?

36 -(Y)E: directional suffix (dative case)

This suffix stands for 'to' and 'for' in English. It indicates a direction:
either a movement towards something or some place, or an action
directed towards a person or thing.

Sinemaya gittik. We went to the cinema.

Ali Ankara'ya gitti. Ali went to Ankara.
Kitabı ona verdim. I gave the book to her.
Bunu size aldım. I bought this for you.
Bize ne getirdiniz? What did you bring for us?

Certain verbs always take the **-(Y)E** suffix: for example, **Duvara baktım** literally means 'I looked to the wall', but the English translation is 'at': 'I looked at the wall'. Similarly, **başlamak** always goes with **-(Y)E**:

Derse başladım. I began the lesson.
Kitaba başladık. We started the book.

The verb **koymak** 'to put' also takes **-(Y)E,** because the action denoted by this verb is a movement from one position to another:

Çiçekleri vazoya koydum. I put the flowers in (lit. to) the vase.
Kitabı masaya koydun mu? Did you put the book on (lit. to) the table?
İskemleye oturdum. I sat down on the chair. (indicates the motion of lowering oneself on to the chair)
İskemlede oturdum. I sat on the chair. (no motion implied)

37 Pronouns in the dative

The vowel in the pronouns **ben** and **sen** changes when they take the dative suffix.

bana	to me	**buna**	to this
sana	to you	**şuna**	to that
ona	to him/her/it	**ona**	to that
bize	to us		
size	to you		
onlara	to them		

Bunu sana vermediler mi? Didn't they give this to you?
Şuna baktım, ama buna bakmadım. I looked at that, but I didn't look at this.

38 Interrogatives in the dative

kime to whom – pl. **kimlere**
Çiçeği kime verdiniz? To whom did you give the flowers?

Kitapları kimlere verdi? To whom (pl.) did he give the books?

neye to what – pl. **nelere**

Neye baktın? What did you look at? (lit. To what did you look?)
(**neye** can also mean 'why', and can also be written as **niye,** where the meaning is rather like 'what for?')

nereye to where – pl. **nerelere** to which places
Dün nereye gittiniz? Where (To where) did you go yesterday?
Çantayı nereye bıraktın? Where (To where) did you leave the bag?
(meaning: Where did you put it?)
Ayşe'yi nerelere götürdünüz? To which places did you take Ayşe?

39 Compound verbs

Quite a large number of Turkish verbs are formed by adding the verb **etmek** to nouns:

teşekkür thanks	**teşekkür etmek** to thank
yardım help	**yardım etmek** to help
seyahat travel	**seyahat etmek** to travel
hücum attack	**hücum etmek** to attack
telefon telephone	**telefon etmek** to telephone
dikkat attention	**dikkat etmek** to pay attention

The nouns used in these compound forms are mostly not Turkish in origin but borrowed from Persian, Arabic or a European language. Some of these nouns undergo a change when used in a compound, and in such cases the compound verb is written as a single word.

af forgiveness	**affetmek** to forgive
his feeling	**hissetmek** to feel
kayıp loss	**kaybetmek** to lose

Some nouns are combined with the verb **olmak** 'to become', 'to be':

kaybetmek to lose	**kaybolmak** to be lost, get lost
memnun etmek to please	**memnun olmak** to be pleased
ziyan etmek to waste	**ziyan olmak** to be wasted

52

The verb **kılmak** meaning 'to do', 'to make' also has a restricted use in forming compounds:

mümkün kılmak to make possible

$$\left.\begin{array}{l}\textbf{etkili}\\\textbf{etkisiz}\end{array}\right\}\ \textbf{kılmak} \qquad \text{to render} \left\{\begin{array}{l}\text{effective}\\\text{ineffective}\end{array}\right.$$

The verb **eylemek** 'to make' is now restricted to a few expressions, having been replaced by **etmek**, and is mostly heard in the set expression **Allah rahmet eylesin**, 'May God have mercy on him/her', with reference to the dead.

Vocabulary

iş	work, job
çarşı	shopping area, bazaar
çarşıya çıkmak	to go shopping
	(to go out to the shops)
alışveriş	shopping
dönmek	to go back, return
seyretmek	to watch
yatak	bed
sonra	later

READING

Dün sabah geç kalktım, işe gitmedim; çarşıya çıktım, alışveriş yaptım. Beyaz, büyük bir çanta aldım, sonra eve döndüm. Ekmek, peynir, meyve yedim. Televizyonda güzel bir film seyrettim ve yattım. Yatakta kitap okudum, sonra uyudum.

Exercise 12

Translate into English:
1 Çocuğu hastaneye götürdüm.
2 Pencereleri kapadı, kapıyı açtı.
3 Biz sütlü çay içtik, onlar meyveli dondurma yedi.
4 Kırmızı çantayı Ayşe'ye verdim, o da bana bu kitabı verdi.
5 Kime telefon ettiniz?
6 Ağır kitapları masaya koymadım, yere koydum.

Lesson 5

40 -DEN: from (ablative case)

This suffix corresponds to the English 'from', 'out of', 'off'. It has four variants: **-den, -dan, -ten, -tan.**

Uçak İzmir'den geldi. The plane came from Izmir.
Trenden indik, otobüse bindik. We got off the train and got on the bus.
Evden çıkmadım. I did not go out of the house.
Kitabı Cemil'den aldım. I got the book from Cemil.

Some verbs go with the ablative:

O adamdan korkmuyorum. I am not afraid of that man.

Interrogatives also take the **-DEN** suffix:

kimden from whom
Mektup kimden geldi? From whom did the letter come?
neden from what (but generally used in the sense of 'why')
Neden gittiler? Why did they go?
Neden para almadın? Why didn't you take (any) money?
nereden from where
Tren nereden geldi? Where did the train come from?
Bu paltoyu nereden aldınız? From where did you buy this coat?

Similarly, pronouns take the **-DEN** suffix quite regularly:
Benden para istedi. He wanted money off me.
Kitapları bizden aldı, onlara verdi. He took the books from us, and gave them to them.
Şundan da yediniz mi? Did you eat some of that too?

41 Interrogatives: hangi 'which' and niçin 'why'

Hangi means 'which':

Hangi çocuk hasta? Which child is ill?
Hangi akşam geldiler? Which evening did they arrive (come)?
Hangi odada oturdunuz? In which room did you sit?

53

Niçin means 'why'. It is a contraction of **ne + için**: 'what for'.

Tren niçin durdu? Why did the train stop?
Bu kitabı niçin okumadınız? Why did you not read this book?

As you know, **neden** and **niye/neye** also mean 'why', and they can all be used interchangeably without changing the meaning at all; **niye/neye** is the more colloquial form and is not used in formal written Turkish.

42 -(N)İN: of (genitive case)

The meaning of the genitive suffix is roughly 'of', and its use approximates to that of the 's in English. It indicates that the noun which takes the genitive ending is the possessor of something, that it possesses something else. Usually the thing it possesses is another noun or noun phrase that comes later in the sentence and carries the possessive suffix (see section 43 below). In English, when you say 'Janet's' or 'the cat's', it implies that Janet and the cat are possessors of something which is either to be mentioned or has already been referred to:

Janet's house   the cat's tail
or
Whose house? Janet's.   Whose tail? The cat's.

The situation is similar in Turkish, except that the thing possessed carries the possessive ending, as we shall see next. Here are some examples with the genitive ending:

Ankara'nın   Ankara's
İstanbul'un Istanbul's
evin   of the house (the house's)
kedinin   the cat's

Pronouns in the genitive show some variations, so here is a list of them:

benim	my	**bizim**	our
senin	your	**sizin**	your
onun	his, her, its	**onların**	their

The interrogatives **kim** and **ne** take the genitive case ending as they take other case endings: **kimin** 'whose', **neyin** 'of what' (note the exception with **neyin: ne** ends in a vowel, so you would expect to have **nenin**, but it is always **neyin**).

Bu kalem kimin? Whose is this pencil?
O kalem benim. That pencil is mine.
O oda senin mi? Is that room yours?
Hayır, o oda benim değil, Ayşe'nin. No, that room is not mine, it is
Ayşe's.
Bu kapak kutunun, ama şu kapak kovanın(dır). This lid is the
box's, but that lid is the bucket's.

The variants for **-(N)İN** are: **-nin, -nın, -nün, nun** after vowels, and
-in, -ın, -ün, -un after consonants.

43 The possessive

The possessive suffixes are different for each person (and each of them
has variants which change according to harmony).

1st person	**-(İ)M**
2nd person	**-(İ)N**
3rd person	**-(S)İ(N)*** (s is the buffer when the base ends in a vowel)
1st person pl.	**-(İ)MİZ**
2nd person pl.	**-(İ)NİZ**
3rd person pl.	**-LERİ(N)***

*The final **N** which is shown in brackets for the 3rd person singular and
plural is used when another case suffix (that is, **-DE, -DEN, -(Y)E,
-(Y)İ** or **-(N)İN**) follows:

bahçeleri their garden
bahçelerinde in their garden
Odası güzel. His room is nice.
Odasında koltuk yok. There is no armchair in his room.

Examples with the possessive suffix:

evim my house		**odam** my room	
evin your house		**odan** your room	
evi his/her/its house		**odası** his room	
evimiz our house		**odamız** our room	
eviniz your house		**odanız** your room	
evleri their house		**odaları** their room	

The possessive suffix indicates that the word to which it is added is
possessed/owned by some other person, thing, etc. mentioned or implied
earlier in the sentence, the word for which carries the genitive suffix.

56

Therefore the word with the genitive suffix can be called the 'possessor' and the one with the possessive suffix can be called the 'possessed'. So in Turkish, when you want to make phrases like 'the teacher's house', you put the possessor (in this case the teacher) first, with the genitive suffix, and the possessed/owned (in this case the house) afterwards, with the possessive suffix. You must remember that in English only one of the words takes a suffix, 's, but in Turkish both words have a suffix. So the phrase 'the teacher's house' is **öğretmenin evi.**

my father's car **babamın arabası**
baba father
babam my father
babamın arabası (lit. my father's, his car)

In English, when you use 'of' instead of 's, the order of the words changes: 'the house of the teacher'/'the teacher's house'. In Turkish the order is always fixed: first the genitive, then the possessive.

In English the possessor and the possessed can be separated by a number of words that describe the possessed (in this case, 'house'):

the teacher's big but rather shabby-looking stone and brick built house

Similarly in Turkish all the words that describe the possessed (in this case **evi**) come before it and thus separate it from the possessor (in this case **öğretmenin**). The translation of the above phrase is:

öğretmenin büyük fakat biraz eski görünüşlü, taş ve tuğladan yapılmış evi

If a Turkish sentence contains a noun with a genitive suffix, then there must be a noun with a possessive suffix later in the same sentence. Sometimes you may only find a possessive suffix, but no genitive before it in the sentence. In such cases it means that the genitive is hidden: it may be a pronoun which has not been explicitly included, but the meaning of which is clearly understood, or it may have been mentioned in the previous sentence and therefore not repeated. But whatever the actual form, the meaning and the implication of the genitive is always there.

Otel çok rahat: odaları büyük ve temiz, plajı çok geniş ve kumlu, bahçesi çok sakin.
The hotel is very comfortable: its rooms are big and clean, its beach is very wide and sandy, its garden is very quiet.

In the Turkish sentence above there is no genitive suffix, although there are three possessive suffixes: **odaları, plajı and bahçesi,** all these linked to 'its' – it being the hotel which was referred to in the first part of the sentence. Indeed, to emphasise the link between **otel** and **odaları, plajı, bahçesi** we could put **onun** before each of these words. But this would be redundant: **onun** is a hidden pronoun there, being present only in sense, not in form. And remember, when the third person possessive is followed by a case suffix, we insert the buffer **N** which has been shown in brackets (see page 55):

Otelin bahçesinde güzel çiçekler var.
Arabanın kapısını açtım.

In colloquial speech it is possible to omit the possessive suffix when there is a pronoun in the genitive:

bizim ev our house
senin çocuk your child

The grammatical rules we have had so far require these to be **bizim evimiz** and **senin çocuğun.** Nevertheless native speakers use the simpler forms, but for you at this stage it is best to keep to the rules.

At these early stages of learning the language you may at times find some ambiguity regarding certain suffixes; for instance, the third person plural possessive suffix **-LERİ(N)** can stand for different things:

kitapları his books   (kitap + lar + ı)
kitapları their book
their books   } (kitap + ları)

As the **-LER** ending cannot be used twice in the same word, we cannot know by looking at the word alone whether it is the book or the possessor that is plural. However, often the context will clarify the ambiguity.

Here are some more straightforward examples:

odanın penceresi the window of the room
kadının çocuğu the woman's child
plajın kumu the sand of the beach
Türkiye'nin başkenti the capital of Turkey

Location

Some nouns indicating locations are often used in genitive-possessive constructions. In English, these are generally called prepositions and are placed before nouns:

ön front
Evin önünde kırmızı bir araba var. There is a red car in front of the house (lit. at the front of the house).
Ayşe'nin önünde kim var? Who is in front of Ayşe?

arka back, behind
Otelin arkasında büyük bir otopark var. There is a large car park behind (lit. at the back of) the hotel.
Arkamda beş kişi var. There are five people behind me.
Ceketini kapının arkasına astı. He hung his jacket behind (lit. to the back of) the door.

alt bottom, under
Masanın altında kediler var. There are cats under the table.
Ağacın altında oturduk. We sat under the tree.

üst top, above
Masanın üstü boş. The top of the table is empty. (i.e. There is nothing on top of the table.)
Tabakları masanın üstüne koydum. I put the plates on (the top of) the table.
The word **üzer-** (always followed by a suffix) is also used for **üst**.

iç interior, inside
Kutunun içi boş. The inside of the box is empty.
Evin içinde kaç kişi var? How many people are there inside the house?

dış exterior, outside
Otelin dışı çok güzel ama içi değil. The exterior (outside) of the hotel is very nice, but the interior (inside) is not.
Kentin dışında büyük parklar var. There are large parks outside the town.
Dışında is also used to mean 'apart from', 'other than':
Bunun dışında bir sorun yok. There is no problem other than this.

yan side, beside
Şişeyi bardağın yanına koyduk. We put the bottle beside the glass.
Çocuk yanıma geldi. The child came near me (lit. to my side).

karşı opposite
Evin karşısında okul var. There is a school opposite the house.

Yemeklerde karşında kim var? Who is opposite you during (at)
meals?

Exercise 13

Translate:
1 Bu sabah evin önünden çok araba geçti.
2 Otelin plajında yüzmedik.
3 Beyaz dolapların içi boş değil.
4 Yaşlı adamın genç arkadaşı onu istasyona götürdü.
5 Otelinizin karşısında ne var?
6 There isn't a garden behind (at the back of) the house.
7 We did not smoke inside the chemist's.
8 The soap and the towels are in the cupboard.
9 There isn't (any) hot water in our room.
10 In Bodrum, which hotel did you stay at?

44 Possessive compounds

When two nouns come together and the first one describes the second,
only the second noun takes the possessive suffix (third person). This
possessive compound represents one single thing. In English neither of
them take any suffix. Remember, the relationship between the two
words is not possession, but description.

diş fırçası toothbrush
el bagajı hand luggage
yatak odası bedroom
elma ağacı apple tree
yüzme havuzu swimming pool

Compare:

çocuğun kitabı the child's book (the book belonging to the child)
çocuk kitabı children's book (book written for children)
bahçenin kapısı the gate of the garden (gate that belongs to the garden)
bahçe kapısı garden gate (a type of gate used for gardens)

You will notice the possessive compound in the names of restaurants,
hotels and banks:

Konyalı Lokantası	the Konyalı Restaurant
Palmiye Oteli	the Palm Tree Hotel
Hilton Oteli	the Hilton Hotel
İş Bankası	the İş Bank

The possessive ending is however omitted in some place names that have been used in that form over the years: **Topkapı, Çengelköy, Arnavutköy, Kadıköy.**

In a possessive compound nothing can come between the components of the compound; any modifiers like an adjective or the indefinite article **bir** come before the entire compound.

küçük, yeşil bir bahçe kapısı a small, green garden gate

In a possessive compound the first element of the compound is more strongly stressed.

A possessive compound can be possessed by another noun carrying the genitive suffix:
çocuğun yatak odası the child's bedroom
or it can form another compound:
misafir yatak odası guest bedroom

In both of these examples **yatak odası** has only one possessive suffix although one expects two possessive suffixes: one for forming the compound **yatak odası,** and then another, in the first example to relate the whole compound to the genitive in **çocuğun,** and in the second to form a compound with **misafir.** This is because there can only be one possessive suffix on any word at one time: what will normally be the last of these possessives is kept and the rest are dropped. Hence, when you want to say 'my bedroom', it is not **yatak odasım** but **yatak odam: sı** is dropped.

El bagajın ağır mı? Is your hand luggage heavy?
Diş fırçanız nerede? Where is your toothbrush?

45 'to have' (possessive + var: has/have)

There is no verb 'to have' in Turkish; its function is carried out by a possessive construction acting as the subject of a **var** or **yok** sentence (see sections 21 and 22). For example, **arabam var** means literally 'there is my car', or 'my car exists'. This is used for 'I have a car'.

Otelin plajı var. The hotel has a beach.
Sigaranız var mı? Do you have a cigarette?
Bugün çok işim var. I have a lot of work today.
Çocuğunuz var mı? Do you have children?

The negative is formed with the possessive suffix and **yok**:

Param yok. I have no money.
Otelin yüzme havuzu yok. The hotel does not have a swimming pool.
Bodrum'da arkadaşları yok. They do not have friend(s) in Bodrum.

46 Interrogatives: kimin, neyin 'whose', 'of what'

The genitive suffix is added to kim and **ne** to mean 'whose', 'who does it belong to' and 'what does it belong to' (see section 18).

Bu kalem kimin? Whose pencil is this?

These interrogatives are used in possessive constructions:

Kimin kalemi yeşil? Whose pencil is green?
Kimin adı Ahmet? Whose name is Ahmet?
Neyin rengi yeşil? What is coloured green? (Green is the colour of what?)
Çimenin rengi yeşil. The colour of grass is green.

47 çünkü and onun için: 'because' and 'so'

These words are used to join sentences in a simple way.

Dün denize girmedim, çünkü müzeye gittim. I didn't go in the sea yesterday, because I went to the museum.
Dün müzeye gittim, onun için denize girmedim. Yesterday I went to the museum, so I didn't go in the sea.
Türkiye çok uzak, onun için bir ay kaldım. Turkey is far away, so I stayed a month.
Bugün çok yorgunum, çünkü dün çok çalıştım. I am very tired today, because I worked hard (lit. a lot) yesterday.

48 Adjectives with the possessive

An adjective used without a noun is understood to refer to a noun:

Sarı temiz, yeşil değil. The yellow one is clean, the green one is not.

When an adjective used like this refers to one out of a number of persons or things, the adjective takes the third person possessive suffix.

Sarısı temiz, yeşili değil.

Hangisi ucuz, mavi mi, beyaz mı? Which (of them) is cheaper, the blue or the white?

Hangisini aldın? Which of them did you buy?

aynı same
aynısı the same of it (i.e. the same as that)
Çantasını beğendim, aynısını aldım. I liked her bag, (and) bought the same (of it).

The word **hep**, which is generally translated as 'always' but can also mean 'all', is used with this possessive suffix – **hepsi** – and means 'all of them/it':

Hepsi ne kadar? How much is it all? (all of it)
Hepsine para verdim. I gave (some) money to all of them.

Some words used in this form have acquired standard meanings alongside their usual meaning with the possessive:

biri someone, a person
Kapıya biri geldi. Someone came to the door.
(This can also be **birisi**, with no change in meaning. This avoids confusion with the definite object form, which is also **biri**.)

kimi some (people), some of the people
Kimi denize girdi, kimi kumda oturdu. Some went in the sea, some sat on the sand.
Like **biri**, this can also be **kimisi**.
Kimisi büyük, kimisi küçük. Some of them are big, some of them small.
Although **kimi** and **kimisi** generally refer to people, they have both come to be used for things as well – the context would tell us which.

63

Exercise 14

Translate the following:
1 Yatak odasının kapısını kapadım.
2 Bu fincanların hepsi güzel; siz hangisini aldınız?
3 Otelimizin banyosuz odası yok.
4 I did not see the police car.
5 Where are your guests? Didn't they come?
6 How many children do you have?
7 All of these jackets are nice, but the white one is very expensive.

Vocabulary

müze	museum
ilginç	interesting
hediye	present, gift
şey(ler)	thing(s)

Note: you will also see an alternative plural form of **şey: eşya**, as in:

hediyelik eşya	souvenirs
fazla	much, extra
bulmak	to find
güneş banyosu	sunbathing

CONVERSATION

– Dün ne yaptınız?
– Müzeye gittik. Müzede çok ilginç şeyler gördük.
– Müze büyük mü?
– Hayır, çok büyük değil; biz hepsini iki saatte gördük. Müzenin yanında küçük bir dükkan var. Arkadaşlarım oradan hediyelik eşya aldı, ama ben almadım, çünkü fazla param yoktu.
– Nerede yemek yediniz?
– Müzenin arkasında bir lokanta bulduk. Yemekleri çok lezzetli. Peki, siz ne yaptınız?
– Biz denize girdik, kumda oturduk, güneş banyosu yaptık.
– Çok güzel.

Lesson 6

49 Adverbs

Adverbs are words which tell us more about an action; they tell us where the action takes place, how it takes place and when it takes place, and are accordingly called adverbs of place, manner and time.
Almost all Turkish adjectives can be used as adverbs.

Kadın güzel konuştu. The woman spoke well.
Çocuklar çok yavaş yürüdü. The children walked very slowly.
Yemeği çabuk yediniz. You ate (the meal) quickly.
Film yeni başladı. The film has just started.
İstanbul'dan yeni geldik. We have recently come (i.e. returned) from Istanbul.

The demonstrative pronouns **bu, şu, o** can give us adverbs of place when they take certain suffixes.

The suffix **-RE-** added to these pronouns forms the bases **bura-** 'this place', **şura-** 'that place', **ora-** 'that place'. These bases must take a case suffix or a possessive suffix before they can be used as individual words. With the third person possessive suffix we obtain the following nouns:

burası this place   **Burası çok rahat.** This place is very comfortable.
şurası that place   **Şurası temiz.** That place is clean.
orası that place   **Orası soğuk.** That place is cold.

With other persons of the possessive suffix the reference is usually to a part of one's body:

Oran nasıl? How is that part (place) of yours? (How/What do you feel in that part of your body?)
Buram iyi. This part of me is OK.

The most frequent use of the bases **bura-, şura-, ora-** as adverbs is with the suffixes **-DE** (locative), **-(Y)E** (dative) and **-DEN** (ablative):

burada   here, in here
şurada   there, in there

orada   there, in there
Arkadaşlarımız burada kalıyor. Our friends are staying here.
Otobüs şurada duruyor. The bus stops there.

buraya   to here
şuraya   to there
oraya   to there
Oraya gitmedik, şuraya gittik. We did not go there, we went there/here.

buradan   from here
şuradan   from there
oradan   from there
Mektup oradan geldi. The letter came from there.

In colloquial speech, the vowel before the suffixes in the above bases is regularly dropped; this can happen in an informal style of writing as well, giving us the forms **burda, şurda, orda, nerde**. However, the correct spelling does keep the vowel, and this is the form you should use in writing.

As we saw above the interrogative **ne** can also take the suffix **-RE-** forming **nere-**; this can then take the possessive suffix and all the case suffixes:

neresi   which place
nerede   where (at where)
nereye   to where
nereden   from where

The above bases can also take the suffixes **-(Y)İ** (definite object) and **-(N)İN** (genitive).

burayı   this place
şurayı   that place
orayı   that place
nereyi   where (which place)
Burayı bilmiyorum. I do not know this place.
İzmir'de nereyi gördün? Which place did you see in Izmir?

buranın   of this place
şuranın   of that place
oranın   of that place
nerenin   of what place

66

Bu ad nerenin? This name is of what place? (belongs to what place?)
Bu anahtar buranın. This key is of this place (belongs to this place).

The following words have a directional meaning; that is, they indicate a direction in which the action takes place. In this sense they can be used as adverbs, whereas in other senses they can function as nouns or adjectives.

içeri	inward, inside
dışarı	outward, outside
ileri	forward
geri	backward
aşağı	downward
yukarı	upward
beri	this way, here

Asansör yukarı çıktı. The lift went up.
Kapıyı içeri ittim. I pushed the door inwards.

They are frequently used with the suffixes **-DE**, **-(Y)E** and **-DEN**; with the **-(Y)E** suffix, however, the direction indicated does not change and therefore the meaning does not change. For this reason it is common practice to leave out this ending.

Araba geri gitti.
Araba geriye gitti. } The car went backwards.

The words **öte** 'further, there' and **karşı** 'across, opposite' are used adverbially with these same suffixes.

Yeşil ışıkta karşıya geçtim. I went across (crossed to the other side) at the green light.
Biraz öteye gitti. He went (moved) a little further.

The direction words listed above are sometimes used in pairs to indicate a two-way motion; the word **bir** often accompanies each word:

Arabalar bir ileri bir geri gitti. The cars went one step forwards, one step backwards. (i.e. very slowly, continually stopping and starting)
Genç adam bir aşağı bir yukarı yürüdü. The young man walked up and down (the street).

The combination **aşağı yukarı** means 'approximately', 'about' and not 'up and down':

İstanbul'da aşağı yukarı bir ay kaldım. I stayed in Istanbul approximately/about a month.

The combination **öte beri** means 'this and that':

Çarşıya çıktım, öte beri aldım. I went shopping, (and) bought this and that.

There are other ways to use words adverbially, as you will see later on in the course (sections 104 and 137).

50 bazı, her, hepsi: 'some', 'every', 'all of it/them'

The word **bazı** has a plural meaning, and the noun following it should be in the plural.

Marmaris'te bazı günler plaja gittim, bazı günler havuza girdim. In Marmaris on some days I went to the beach, and on some days I went in the pool.

Bazı turistler yemekleri sevmedi. Some tourists did not like the food.

You can omit the plural noun and just put the plural suffix with a possessive suffix after **bazı:**

Bazıları yemekleri sevmedi. Some (people) did not like the food.

When 'some' is used to refer to an 'uncounted' amount we use **biraz**, which also means 'a little', especially when used as an adverb:

Biraz çalıştım. I worked a little/a bit.
Biraz viski içtik. We had some whisky.
Bankadan biraz para aldım. I took some money from the bank.

When 'some' has a singular meaning, we use **bir**:
bir gün   some day
bir şey   something
bir yer   somewhere
Çantamı bir yerde bıraktım. I left my bag somewhere.

The word **her** means 'every':

Hergün yüzdük. We swam every day.
Her şeyi anladım. I understood everything.

And **herkes** means 'everyone':

Herkes burada mı? Is everyone here?

'All of it' or 'all of them' is **hepsi**:

Filmin hepsini gördüm. I saw all of the film.
Kağıtların hepsi masanın üstünde. All of the papers are on the table.

The word **bütün** is also used to mean 'all', but it is used as an adjective and always comes before a noun:

Bütün kağıtlar masanın üstünde. All the papers are on the table.
Bütün gün çalıştık. We worked all day.

Another word meaning 'all' is **tüm.** It can be used as an adjective or as a noun. When used as a noun it takes the possessive ending.

Tüm pencereleri açtım. I opened all the windows.
Pencerelerin tümünü açtım. I opened all of the windows.

The word **hiç** in various combinations is used for the negative of the expressions above:

hiç kimse no one   **kimse** anyone
hiç bir zaman never
hiç bir şey nothing

Hiç used with negatives means 'none', 'never', 'none at all':

Hiç yemedim. I never ate.
İstanbul'a hiç gitmedim. I have never been to Istanbul.
Hiç yemek yok. There is no food at all.
Plajda kimse var mı? Is there anyone on the beach?
Hayır, hiç kimse yok. No, there is no one at all.

51 İDİ/-(Y)Dİ: the past form of 'to be'

İDİ is seldom used as a separate word by itself; in written and spoken Turkish it is used as a suffix equivalent to the past tense of 'to be'. The suffix form can be represented as **-(Y)Dİ:** after bases that end in a vowel it is **-ydi, -ydı, -ydü** or **-ydu**, after the voiceless consonants **p, t, k, ç, s, ş, f, h**, it is **-ti, -tı, -tü, -tu**, and after all other consonants it is **-di, -dı, -dü, -du.** It is followed by the same personal suffixes as the past tense suffix **-Dİ.**

Dün çok yorgundum. Yesterday I was very tired.
Sen evdeydin ama kardeşin okuldaydı. You were at home, but your
brother/sister was at school.
Adam Türktü. The man was Turkish.
Kadın Londralıydı. The woman was a Londoner.
Hastaydık. We were ill.
Otelimiz çok rahattı. Our hotel was very comfortable.
Hava çok kötüydü. The weather was very bad.

İDİ is also used with **var** and **yok** to mean 'there was' and 'there was
not':

Masada iki kitap vardı. There were two books on the table.
Odada koltuk yoktu. There was no armchair in the room.
Evde yoktu. He was not at home.
Partide kimler vardı? Who (pl) were at the party?

With the genitive + **var/yok**, **İDİ** means had/had not (did not have):
Param vardı ama vaktim yoktu. I had money, but I did not have
time.
İşimiz vardı, onun için plaja gitmedik. We had things to do, so we
did not go to the beach.

52 Question forms with -(Y)Dİ

-(Y)Dİ comes between the question marker **Mİ** and the personal
endings:

Dün evde miydin? Were you at home yesterday?
Otelde miydiler? Were they at the hotel?
Hasta mıydık? Were we ill?
Geçen yaz Marmaris'te miydiniz? Were you in Marmaris last
summer?
Otelinizin havuzu yok muydu? Didn't your hotel have a pool?

If the question is formed with an interrogative, then that interrogative
carries the **-(Y)Dİ** suffix provided it is not the subject:

Çocuklar neredeydi? (lit. The *children* (subject) were where?) Where
were the children?
O kimdi? (lit. *He/she/it* (subject) was who?) Who was it?
Mektup kimdendi? (lit. *The letter* (subject) was from whom?) Who
was the letter from?

Note that in the last three sentences above, the subject and the word order are the reverse of what is most natural in English. Thus 'He was who?' rather than 'Who was he?' (see section 18).

53 Negatives with -(Y)Dİ

Değil takes the past suffix -(Y)Dİ, and then comes the personal ending:

Plajda değildik çünkü hava kötüydü. We weren't on the beach, because the weather was bad.
Otobüste değildim, dolmuştaydım. I was not on the bus, I was in the dolmuş.
Hasta değildi, yorgundu. He was not ill, he was tired.

54 Negative questions with -(Y)Dİ

The order of the endings is as follows:

— + değil + Mİ + (Y)Dİ + person
Hava güzel değil miydi? Wasn't the weather nice?
Evde değil miydiniz? Weren't you at home?

-(Y)Dİ can also be added to tense suffixes. It then forms a compound tense with a past reference. Examples are given with each tense in later lessons. It is seldom used after -Dİ (past).

Exercise 15

Translate the following:
1 Orası çok güzel bir yer; Londra'dan otuz kişi geldi ve orada on beş gün kaldı.
2 Araba ileri gitmedi, geri gitti.
3 Bu anahtar nerenin?
4 Cuma günü çok hastaydım, doktora gittim.
5 Dün akşam size telefon ettim, odanızda değildiniz.
6 He spoke very fast, I did not understand.
7 This is a very nice place.
8 How many people stayed here?

9 Did the bus stop here?
10 In Istanbul the weather was very hot every day.

55 Days of the week

Pazar	Sunday	**Perşembe**	Thursday
Pazartesi	Monday	**Cuma**	Friday
Salı	Tuesday	**Cumartesi**	Saturday
Çarşamba	Wednesday		

yarın	tomorrow
öbür gün	the day after tomorrow
ertesi gün	the following day
evvelki } **gün** **evvelsi**	the day before yesterday
hafta	week
geçen hafta	last week
gelecek hafta	next week
öbür hafta	the week after next
ertesi hafta	the following week
ay	month
yıl } **sene**	year

In English you say 'on Tuesday', 'on Friday', etc.; in Turkish we just say
Salı 'Tuesday', or **Salı günü** '(day of) Tuesday', **Perşembe akşamı**
'Thursday evening'.

Salı günü sinemaya gittik. We went to the cinema on Tuesday.
or
Salı sinemaya gittik, Çarşamba tiyatroya gittik. On Tuesday we
  went to the cinema, on Wednesday we went to the theatre.

The plural can also be used:

Salı günleri dükkanlar kapalı. The shops are closed on Tuesdays.
Cuma akşamları otelde disko var. There is a disco in the hotel on
  Friday evenings.
Pazarları dükkanlar çok kalabalık. The shops are very crowded on
  Sundays.

72

To say 'in the morning' you do not use the suffix **-DE** 'in, on, at'; it is
either just **sabah** or **sabahleyin**. Similarly:

öğleyin	at noon
akşam/akşamleyin	in the evening
gece/geceleyin	at night
sabahları	in the mornings
öğleleri	at noon times
akşamları	in the evenings
geceleri	at nights

Various times of any day of the week are expressed as compounds:

Cumartesi gecesi	Saturday night
Pazar sabahı	Sunday morning

**Gelecek hafta Cumartesi gecesi saat onda televizyonda iyi bir
film var.** There is a good film on TV next week on Saturday night
at ten o'clock.

But 'on Sunday, in the morning' is **Pazar (günü) sabah** or **Pazar
(günü) sabahleyin.**

Çarşamba günü sabahleyin saat onda randevum var. I have an
appointment on Wednesday in the morning at 10 o'clock.

56 Months

Ocak	January	**Temmuz**	July
Şubat	February	**Ağustos**	August
Mart	March	**Eylül**	September
Nisan	April	**Ekim**	October
Mayıs	May	**Kasım**	November
Haziran	June	**Aralık**	December

Ağustos'ta Türkiye'de hava çok sıcaktır.
In August the weather is very hot in Turkey.
Mayıs'ta tatile gittiler.
They went on holiday in May.

When giving dates with months we use cardinal numbers:

dokuz Şubat nine February
yirmi bir Mart twenty-one March

or we can say

Şubat'ın dokuzu the ninth of February
Mart'ın yirmi biri the twenty-first of March
Bugün on sekiz Eylül 1989. Today is 18 September 1989.
Bugün Eylül'ün on sekizi. Today is the eighteenth of September.
(In the second type of structure the year is not given.)

57 Seasons

mevsim	season
ilkbahar	spring (**bahar** alone can also mean 'spring')
yaz	summer
sonbahar	autumn
kış	winter

Exercise 16

Translate the following:
1 Last year we weren't in Turkey.
2 At noon, the shops are not closed, but the banks are closed.
3 We go to the cinema on Friday evenings.
4 Where were you on Thursday?
5 I read all of the book.

Vocabulary

dolmuş	a shared taxi		**geniş**	wide
vakit	time		**yemek**	food, meal
zaman	time			(dinner/lunch)
çabuk	quickly		**banyo**	bathroom
yavaş	slowly		**duş**	shower
çimen	grass		**garson**	waiter
deniz kıyısı	seaside, seashore		**servis**	service
kıyı	shore		**tatil**	holiday
bahçe	garden			

READING

Geçen ay Marmaris'e gittik. Otelimiz deniz kıyısındaydı. Otelin büyük bir bahçesi ve geniş bir plajı vardı. Plaj çok güzeldi. Otelin yemekleri de çok güzeldi; garsonlar ve servis çok iyiydi. Her odada banyo ya da duş vardı. Bazı akşamlar radyoyu açtık ve müzik dinledik. Otelimizin karşısında küçük bir ada vardı; bir gün o adaya gittik, orada denize girdik. Marmaris'te on beş gün kaldık ve çok güzel bir tatil yaptık.

Lesson 7

58 The present continuous tense: -(İ)YOR

This tense is used to indicate action going on at the time of speaking. It is also used for habitual action, action done repeatedly as a routine, and also for future action, especially when used in the company of words referring to the future, like 'tomorrow' or 'next year'. It corresponds to the 'am/is/are ...ing' tense in English and also to the English present and future.

The basic form of this tense is -(İ)YOR. The -yor part of the suffix never changes; it never harmonises with what comes before it. When the verb base ends in a vowel, the tense suffix is just -yor, e.g. okuyor, yürüyor, kuruyor. When the verb base ends in a consonant, the tense suffix is -İYOR; its variants are -iyor, -ıyor, -üyor, -uyor. For example: geliyor, bakıyor, gülüyor, buluyor.

The personal suffixes that are used with -(İ)YOR are the same personal suffixes that represent the present form of 'to be' (see section 12). The personal suffixes that follow the tense ending -(İ)YOR also never change, -yor being always constant:

first person	-um
second person	-sun
third person	—
first person plural	-uz
second person plural	-sunuz
third person plural	(-lar)

The order of the suffixes is as follows:

verb + (İ)YOR + person

gel	iyor	um	geliyorum	I am coming/I come
oku	yor	sun	okuyorsun	you are reading/you read

Türkçe öğreniyorum. I am learning Turkish.
Bu akşam sinemaya gidiyoruz. We are going to the cinema this evening.

When the verb base ends in **e** or **a**, these vowels become **i** and **ı** respectively before the **-yor** suffix:

ye	+ yor	= yiyor	he eats/is eating
de	+ yor	= diyor	he says/is saying
anla	+ yor	= anlıyor	he understands
bekle	+ yor	= bekliyor	he waits/is waiting

59 Negative with -(İ)YOR

The negative suffix **-me** or **-ma** precedes **-(İ)YOR**:

verb	+ negative	+ (İ)YOR	+ person	
gel	me	yor	um	gelmiyorum I am not coming
oku	ma	yor	um	okumuyorum I am not reading

Notice the sound change in the negative suffix before the **-yor** suffix: **me** becomes **mi**, and **ma** becomes **mı**; if the vowel before the negative suffix is round, then the negative suffix becomes **mü** or **mu**. For example:

gül + **me** + **yor** = **gülmüyor**   he is not laughing
oku + **ma** + **yor** = **okumuyor**   he is not reading
Bu yaz Bodrum'a gitmiyoruz. We are not going to Bodrum this
  summer.
Uçak beşte kalkıyor. The plane leaves at five.

60 Questions with -(İ)YOR

The question marker **Mİ** is placed after **-(İ)YOR** and before the personal suffix:*

verb	+ (İ)YOR	+ question	+ person
gel	iyor	mu	yum
geliyor muyum? am I coming?			
öğren	iyor	mu	sunuz
öğreniyor musunuz? are you learning?			
al	ıyor	mu	yuz
alıyor muyuz? are we buying?			
Türkçe öğreniyor mu? Is he learning Turkish?			

*With the third person plural suffix the **Mİ** question marker comes

after the person:
Geliyorlar mı? Are they coming?
İngilizce biliyorlar mı? Do they know (speak) English?

Remember, when there is a question word, the question marker **Mİ** is *not* used:

Niçin ağlıyorlar? Why are they crying?
Arkadaşının hediyesini ne zaman veriyorsun? When are you
giving (going to give) your friend's present?
Nerede oturuyorlar? Where do they live?
Nereye gidiyoruz? Where are we going?

61 Negative questions with -(İ)YOR

All the suffixes follow each other in the positions described:

verb + negative + **(İ)YOR** + question + person
bak   ma   yor   mu   yum
bakmıyor muyum? aren't I looking?
gör   me   yor   mu   sun
görmüyor musun? aren't you seeing (don't you see)?
Çocuklara kitap vermiyor musunuz? Aren't you giving books to
the children?
Burada oturmuyorlar mı? Aren't they living here (Don't they live
here)?

62 The past continuous tense

The suffix **-(Y)Dİ**, the past form of 'to be', can be added to the present
continuous suffix **-(İ)YOR** to form the past continuous, in English
'was/were ...ing'. It indicates continuous action happening in the past.

Araba çok hızlı gidiyordu, birden lastik patladı.
The car was going very fast, suddenly the tyre burst.
Rüyamda İstanbul'a gidiyordum.
In my dream I was going (travelling) to Istanbul.

-(Y)Dİ forms this kind of compound tense with all the other tenses as
well.

63 İLE: with, by, by means of, through

İLE may be used as a separate word meaning 'with, by, by means of, through', but more frequently it is used as a suffix and can be shown as -(Y)LE:

1   If the word ends in a vowel, the suffix is -yle or -yla:
    arabayla   by car
    öğrenciyle   with the student
    kediyle   with the cat
    neyle   with what, by what
2   If the word ends in a consonant, the suffix is either -le or -la:
    trenle   by train
    uçakla   by plane (also 'by air mail')
    adamla   with the man

Türkiye'ye trenle üç günde gittim. I went to Turkey by train in three days.
Arabayla bir saatte gidiyoruz. By car we go (get there) in one hour.
Hesabı çekle ödedim. I paid the bill by cheque.
Marmaris'e neyle gidiyorsunuz? How (By what) are you going to Marmaris?
Adamla konuşmadım, kadınla konuştum.
I didn't speak to (with) the man, I spoke to (with) the woman.

İLE is also used to mean 'and' where it implies a togetherness, for instance:

Ahmetle Mehmet bu akşam bize geliyor. Ahmet and Mehmet are coming (together) to (see) us tonight.
Ekmekle peynir yedik. We ate bread and cheese.
Havluyla mayoyu aldım. I took the towel and the bathing suit.

Note that the object suffix has been omitted in **havluyla**: İLE does not follow case suffixes, but it can be used with the possessive suffix. For instance:

Havlumla mayomu aldım. I took my towel and my bathing suit.
Gömleğimle şortumu giydim. I put on my shirt and shorts.

When İLE is used with a pronoun, the pronoun is always in the genitive form, except the pronouns that end in -LER. The same happens with the interrogative **kim.**

Personal: **benimle** with me
seninle with you
onunla with him/her/it
bizimle with us
sizinle with you (pl/formal)
onlarla with them
Demonstrative: **bununla** with this   **bunlarla** with these
şununla with that   **şunlarla** with those
onunla with that   **onlarla** with those (= with them)
kiminle with whom?   **kimlerle** with whom (pl)?

Bizimle sinemaya geliyor musun? Are you coming to the cinema with us?
Tatile kiminle gidiyorsunuz? With whom are you going on holiday?

Vocabulary

öğrenmek	to learn	**saç**	hair
ağlamak	to weep	**taramak**	to comb
hediye	gift	**elbise**	dress, suit
öğrenci	student	**giymek**	to wear
hesap	bill	**dilim**	slice
çek	cheque	**kızarmış**	toasted, fried
ödemek	to pay	**ekmek**	bread
hızlı	fast	**kızarmış ekmek**	toast
birden	suddenly	**peynir**	cheese
lastik	tyre (of car etc.)	**tereyağ**	butter
patlamak	to burst, explode	**reçel**	jam
rüya ⎱	dream	**yürümek**	to walk
düş ⎰		**Türkiye**	Turkey
erken	early	**Türkçe**	Turkish
kahvaltı	breakfast	**bilmek**	to know
çay	tea	**gömlek**	shirt
sevmek	to like, love	**şort**	shorts
yüz	face	**mayo**	bathing suit,
yıkamak	to wash		swimming
önce	first		trunks

READING

Sabahları erken kalkıyorum. Banyoya giriyorum, yüzümü yıkıyorum, saçımı tarıyorum, elbisemi giyiyorum. Kahvaltıda her zaman çay

80

içiyorum; çayı çok seviyorum ve sütsüz içiyorum. Bir dilim kızarmış ekmek ve peynir yiyorum, tereyağ ve reçel yemiyorum. Sekizde evden çıkıyorum, durağa yürüyorum. İşime otobüsle gidiyorum. Siz kahvaltıda ne yiyorsunuz? İşe neyle gidiyorsunuz?

Exercise 17

Translate the following:
1 We are going to Turkey this year.
2 I don't walk to the station, I get on a bus.
3 We don't know Turkish, but we are learning.
4 Are you coming with us?
5 The children were swimming in the pool.

64 Numerals: ordinal

birinci	first	altıncı	sixth
ikinci	second	yedinci	seventh
üçüncü	third	sekizinci	eighth
dördüncü	fourth	dokuzuncu	ninth
beşinci	fifth	onuncu	tenth

yüzüncü	hundredth
bininci	thousandth
beş yüz otuz sekizinci	five hundred and thirty-eighth

In writing, a full stop is put after a numeral to indicate that it is an ordinal:

12. sayfa	12th page
5. ay	5th month

The ordinal suffix can be used with the interrogative **kaç**, giving us **kaçıncı?** The response is always with an ordinal numeral:

Şubat kaçıncı ay?   **Şubat ikinci ay.**
Which month is February?   February is the second month.
Atınız yarışta kaçıncı geldi?
Where did your horse come in the race?

The ordinal number can also be abbreviated by putting the suffix after the number:

1inci = birinci   1st = first
6ncı = altıncı   6th = sixth

65 Numerals: distributive

The suffix **-(Ş)ER** is added to numerals to form distributive adjectives. When a number ends in a vowel the suffix is **-şer** or **-şar**, as in **ikişer** 'two each' and **altışar** 'six each', and when a number ends in a consonant the distributive suffix becomes **-er** or **-ar**, as in **birer** 'one each' and **onar** 'ten each'.

birer	one each	**yüzer**	a hundred each
ikişer	two each	**beş yüzer**	five hundred each
üçer	three each	**beşer yüz**	
dörder	four each	**biner**	a thousand each
beşer	five each	**on biner**	ten thousand each
altışar	six each	**onar bin**	
yedişer	seven each	**kırk beşer**	forty-five each
sekizer	eight each	**yarımşar**	half each
dokuzar	nine each		
onar	ten each		

Lokantada yarımşar şişe şarap içtik.
We drank half a bottle of wine each at the restaurant.
Her odada ikişer yatak var. There are two beds (each) in every room.

When **buçuk** is used, the number preceding **buçuk** takes the **-(Ş)ER** ending:

ikişer buçuk kilo elma two and a half kilos each of apples

The distributive interrogative is **kaçar** 'how many each?':

Bu gömlekler kaçar lira? How many lira each are these shirts?

Distributive numerals can also be used as adverbs when they are doubled:

Öğrenciler birer birer sınıfa girdi. The students entered the classroom one by one.
Merdivenleri ikişer ikişer çıktık. We climbed the stairs two by two.

The words **tek** 'single' and **az** 'little' can also be used in this way:
Kelimeleri teker teker söylüyor. He is saying the words singly (one by one).
İçkisini azar azar içti. He drank his drink a little at a time.

66 -DEN BERİ: since

This combination indicates that action begun at some specified time is still continuing, so it is mostly used with the **-(İ)YOR** tense marker. The **-DEN** suffix in the combination harmonises in the usual way.

Sabahtan beri çalışıyorum. I have been working (lit. I am working) since the morning.
Saat ondan beri konuşuyorlar. They have been talking since ten o'clock.
Dün akşamdan beri yemek yemedi. He has not eaten since last night.

English uses 'for' (instead of 'since'), if the time denoted is a period of time. In such cases Turkish uses **-DEN BERİ** if the action is still continuing:

Telefon üç günden beri çalışmıyor. The telephone has not been working for three days.

But **-den beri** is not used if the action is no longer continuing:

Telefon üç gün çalışmadı. The telephone did not work for three days.

67 -DİR: for

This suffix is used in the same way as **-den beri**, but only with descriptions of definite periods of time in terms of months, years, days, hours etc.
Telefon üç gündür çalışmıyor. The phone has not been working for three days.

İki haftadır Ayvalık'tayız. We have been in Ayvalık for two weeks.

68 -(Y)E KADAR: up to, until

This combination refers to a limit in time or distance, so it can also mean 'as far as', 'by'.

Beşe kadar bekledik. We waited until five o'clock.
Akşama kadar çalıştınız mı? Did you work until the evening?
İstasyona kadar yürüdük. We walked as far as the station.
İstanbul'a kadar uçakla gidiyoruz, İstanbul'dan İzmir'e otobüsle devam ediyoruz. We are going by plane as far as Istanbul; from Istanbul to Izmir we are going to carry on by coach.
Kitabı beşinci sayfaya kadar okudum. I read the book up to page five.

Interrogatives can also be used with -(y)e kadar:

Kaça kadar? Until when? Up to what number?
Nereye kadar? As far as where?
Ne zamana kadar? Until when?

Kadar without the -(Y)E suffix means 'as much as', or 'about/approximately'.

Bir saat kadar bekledik. We waited for about an hour.
Eylül Ağustos kadar sıcak değil. September is not as hot as (lit. not hot as much as) August.
Altı kilometre kadar yürüdüm. I walked for about six kilometres.

When kadar is used with pronouns, the latter are in the genitive:

Benim kadar yedi. He ate as much as I did.
Sizin kadar Türkçe bilmiyorum. I do not know Turkish as well as you.

With interrogatives:
Ne kadar? How much? (lit. As much as what?)

This phrase is frequently used to ask the price of something:
Bir kilo üzüm ne kadar? How much is a kilo of grapes?

bu kadar this much
o kadar that much, all that

Film o kadar güzel değil. The film is not all that good.

69 -DEN ÖNCE: before

Yemekten önce birer viski içtik. We had a whisky each before dinner.
Ankara'dan önce Konya'ya gittiler. They went to Konya before Ankara.

You may also hear **-DEN EVVEL**, which has the same meaning:

Yemekten evvel birer viski içtik.
Benden evvel sırada kim var? Who is in the queue before me?
Bundan önce neredeydiniz? Where were you before this (previously)?

Used without the **-DEN** suffix, **önce** can mean 'first', 'previously':

Önce Türkçe öğrendim. First, I learnt Turkish.

To indicate a situation which exists *before an action*, the suffix cluster **-MEDEN** is used with **önce** and the combined form is directly added to the verb base: verb + **-MEDEN ÖNCE** = 'before doing something'.

Evden çıkmadan önce pencereleri kapadım. Before leaving the house I closed the windows.

There is no tense or person indicator. If the person is not the subject or doer of the main verb, then it is stated separately:

Arkadaşım gelmeden önce kitaplarımı kaldırdım. I put away my books before my friend came.
Arkadaşım gelmeden önce telefon etti. My friend rang before coming (before she came).
Denize girmeden önce güneşte oturduk. We sat in the sun before going in the sea.
Yatmadan önce bir bardak süt içiyorum. Before going to bed I drink a glass of milk.
Evden çıkmadan önce ne yapıyorsunuz? What do you do before you leave the house (lit. before leaving the house)?

70 -DEN SONRA: after

Yemekten sonra kahve içtik. We drank coffee after dinner.
Antalya'dan sonra Dalaman'a gidiyoruz. We are going to
Dalaman after Antalya.
Bu istasyondan sonra hangi istasyon geliyor? Which station
comes after this station?
Plajdan sonra nereye gidiyorsunuz? Where are you going after the
beach?
Kahvaltıdan sonra yürüyüşe çıkıyoruz. We are going for a walk
after breakfast.

Used without the **-DEN** suffix, **sonra** means 'later', 'then', 'afterwards':

Otele önce mektup yazdım, sonra telefon ettim. First I wrote to
the hotel, then I telephoned.
Önce yağmur, sonra kar yağdı. First it rained, then it snowed.

To indicate a situation *after an action*, the suffix cluster **-DİKTEN** is
used with **sonra** and the combined form is directly added to a verb
base: verb + **-DİKTEN SONRA** = 'after doing something'.

Yemek yedikten sonra kahve içtik. After eating we had coffee.
Siz gittikten sonra Ahmet ve eşi geldi. After you left, Ahmet and
his wife came.
İzmir'e gittikten sonra Bodrum'a gidiyorlar. After going to İzmir,
they are going to Bodrum.

Vocabulary

dolu	full	**içki**	drink (alcoholic)
boş	empty	**sıra**	queue, row
merdiven	stairs	**beklemek**	to wait
kelime	word	**yürüyüş**	a walk
bavul	suitcase	**biraz**	a little

Exercise 18

Translate the following:
1 The first bus was full, so we got on the second bus.
2 We had (drank) two teas each.

3 We have been staying (are staying) in this hotel since last Sunday.
4 I walked as far as the hotel.
5 What did you do after the meal?

71 Forms of address

In addressing people formally in Turkish, the words **bey** 'gentleman' and **hanım** 'lady' are used with the first names:

Günaydın Ahmet Bey. Good morning, Ahmet Bey.
Nasılsınız Ayşe Hanım? How are you, Ayşe Hanım?

If surnames are used, then the words **Bay** 'Mr' or **Bayan** 'Mrs/Miss' precede the surname (and the first name, if one is given) as in English:

Bay Ahmet Atakan or **Bay Atakan**
Bayan Ayşe Kutlu or **Bayan Kutlu**

Another form of address where surnames are used is **Sayın** 'esteemed': it is formal, indicating respect, and is used for both men and women in the same way. It can also be used with titles:

Sayın Profesör Ekin orada mı? Is Professor Ekin there?
Sayın Ayşe Kutlu biraz sonra geliyor. Mrs Ayşe Kutlu will be here a little later (i.e. is coming).
Sayın Başbakan gelecek ay Amerika'ya gidiyor. The Prime Minister is going to America next month.

As all these forms of address indicate a certain degree of formality, the personal suffix to be used with them is of course second person plural:

Sayın Atakan, bu kitabı istiyor musunuz?

You can address an envelope:

    Sayın Ahmet Atakan
or **Bay Ahmet Atakan**
or **Sayın Bay Ahmet Atakan**

but inside, begin the letter:

Sayın Atakan (official letters)
Sayın Müdür/Doktor/etc.
Ahmet Bey/Ayşe Hanım (still formal, but less official, more personal)

The direct translation of the word 'dear' is **sevgili,** but in Turkish this indicates great familiarity and closeness and should be avoided unless you have been addressed as such. There is no danger of offending anyone if you keep to the more formal forms until you gain familiarity.

If you want to address the whole family, you use the form **Sayın Atakan ailesi.** The plural ending **-LER** can also be used with proper names to refer to a person and his family or close circle:

Bu akşam Ayşelere gidiyoruz. We are going to Ayşe's this evening.
Ayşeler burada oturuyor. Ayşe and her family/friends live here.
Atakanların evi nerede? Where is the Atakans' house?

Vocabulary

motor gezisi	boat trip
koy	small bay or cove
buluşmak	to meet
kahvaltı etmek	to have breakfast

CONVERSATION

Telefonda

- Alo, Ayşe, sen misin?
- Merhaba Ahmet, nasılsın?
- Teşekkür ederim, iyiyim. Sen nasılsın?
- Ben de iyiyim.
- Ayşe, yarın motor gezisine gidiyoruz. Geliyorsun, değil mi?
- Tabii geliyorum, ama motor kaçta kalkıyor?
- Sabah onda Büyük Otel'in önünden kalkıyor. Öğle yemeğini küçük bir koyda yedikten sonra üç saat kadar bu koyda kalıyoruz, denize giriyoruz. Çayımızı da orada içtikten sonra Büyük Otel'e dönüyoruz.
- Serpil'le Cengiz de geliyor mu?
- Tabii.
- Peki, nerede buluşuyoruz?
- Saat dokuzda otelde buluşuyoruz, önce kahvaltı ediyoruz.
- Tamam, ben de saat dokuzda oradayım.
- Peki, iyi günler.
- İyi günler.

88

Exercise 19

Translate the following:
1 We are on holiday until September.
2 I lost my ticket before the plane took off, but later I found (it).
3 We opened all the windows before smoking.
4 Last night, after you left, I telephoned London.

Lesson 8

72 Imperatives

The simplest way to form a command is to use the verb without the infinitive **-MEK** suffix:

Buraya gel. Come here.
Bana bir kahve getir. Bring me a coffee.
Aç. Open.

However, this is not the formal way of asking something to be done, neither is it very polite. It is used when speaking to people you address as **sen**. You can always put **lütfen** with it. When speaking to people you address as **siz** (used for both the plural and the formal singular), the more polite form of command, **-(Y)İN** or **-(Y)İNİZ**, is added to the verb. In terms of politeness there is no difference between them, but **-(Y)İN** is more frequently used in spoken Turkish and **-(Y)İNİZ** in written Turkish; this latter suffix you will see a lot on signs and notices, and on all kinds of official communications. For example:

(on a train)	**Pencereden dışarı sarkmayınız.**
	Do not lean out of the window.
(in a library)	**Gürültü etmeyiniz.**
	Do not make a noise.
(on a bus)	**Şoförle konuşmayınız.**
	Do not talk to the driver.
(on a door)	**İtiniz.** Push.
	Çekiniz. Pull.

Being shorter, **-(Y)İN** is more frequent in spoken Turkish:

Yarın akşam erken gelin. Come early tomorrow evening.
İstanbul'da Topkapı müzesini görün. See the Topkapı museum in Istanbul.
Bu sabah iki gazete alın. Buy two newspapers this morning.

You can use **lütfen** in all these sentences to make your request less abrupt, more polite.

For negative imperatives, put the relevant imperative suffix after the negative **-ME**:

Hava güzel, şemsiye almayın. The weather is fine, do not take an umbrella.
Çantanızı burada bırakmayın. Do not leave your bag here.
Bu kutuyu açma. Do not open this box.
Kağıdı yere atma. Do not throw the paper on the floor.

To summarise, a simple rule for which imperative form to use is:

a) Use the plain form of the verb (without any suffixes except the **-ME** ending if the imperative is negative) for people whom you address as **sen**.

b) Use **-(Y)İN** after the verb (or, for the negative, after the verb + **-ME**) for people you address as **siz**. And try to add **lütfen** 'please' as you do in English: you can start your imperative sentence with **lütfen**, or put **lütfen** at the end of the sentence.

Lütfen beşte gel.
Lütfen beşte gelin. } Please come at five.

Beşte gel lütfen.
Beşte gelin lütfen. } Come at five please.

When you are asking for things at a restaurant or a shop, it is quite sufficient to name what you want, coupled with **lütfen**:

Bir çay lütfen. One tea please.
Yarım kilo üzüm lütfen. Half a kilo of grapes please.

In colloquial Turkish there is another way of forming the imperative. It is very frequently used in spoken Turkish, but seldom in writing. The suffix used for this is **-SENE** for people you address as **sen**, and **-SENİZE** for people you address as **siz**.

Çabuk olsana. Be quick. (indicating impatience: Hurry up!)
Kapıyı açsanıza. Open the door.
İçsene. Drink (it).

This form of request is rather abrupt and can indicate some impatience on the part of the person making the request. You would be well advised to avoid using it – but you will often hear it used, particularly when a person addresses a junior colleague or employee.

For another, very polite way to make a request, rather like the English 'Would you...', see section 88.

Yet another suffix used frequently in colloquial speech to form an imperative is **-(Y)İVER**. It is added to a verb and implies that the action indicated by the verb can be done quickly and easily. The suffix is **-(Y)İ + VER**, and only the first vowel harmonises; the second part of the suffix is non-harmonic, it is always **VER**.

Havluları dolaba koyuver. Put the towels in the cupboard.
On dakika bekleyiver. Wait for ten minutes.

In non-imperative sentences **-(Y)İVER** can be followed by all the suffixes that a verb can take, but generally it only takes the tense and person suffixes. It implies that the action can be done, or has been done, quickly and without much fuss.

Çamaşırları soğuk suda yıkayıverdim. I washed the laundry in cold water.
On dakika içinde bavulunu hazırlayıverdi. He got his case ready (lit. prepared his case) in ten minutes.

73 The optative

The suffix used for the optative is **-(Y)E** with a verb base. This form of the verb indicates not an action but a wish, a desire for an action to take place, or for something to happen. Its variants are **-ye, -ya** after vowels and **-e, -a** after consonants. It takes a special set of person endings:

-YİM	I
-SİN	you (sing)
-SİN* or nothing (see below)	he/she/it
-LİM	we
-SİNİZ	you (pl/formal)
-SİNLER or **-LER**	they

*The third person has two forms: either no suffix for the person is used after the optative suffix, or the personal suffix **-SİN** is added directly to the verb base without the optative suffix: **gel-e** or **gel-sin**. The same happens for the third person plural, but the **-LER** suffix is used especially if the subject is left out and is to be understood from the personal suffix of the verb: **gel-e-ler** or **gel-sinler**. Examples:

göreyim	alayım	bekleyeyim
göresin	alasın	bekleyesin
göre/görsün	ala/alsın	bekleye/beklesin
görelim	alalım	bekleyelim
göresiniz	alasınız	bekleyesiniz
göreler/görsünler	alalar/alsınlar	bekleyeler/beklesinler

The optative is mostly used with the first person singular and plural; forms in the other persons are very restricted in usage, except for the third person form with the -SİN suffix.

1 With the first person the most general meaning is 'let me/us...':
Sen yorgunsun, alışverişi ben yapayım. You are tired, let me do the shopping.
Saat beşte geleyim mi? Shall I come at five o'clock? (the person asking the question wants to come at five and is seeking agreement)
Geç oldu, ben gideyim. It's late, I'd better go (let me go).
Biraz daha bekleyelim mi? Shall we wait a little longer?
Bu akşam sinemaya gidelim. Let's go to the cinema tonight.
Havaalanına taksiyle gidelim, çok pahalı değil. Let's go to the airport by taxi, it's not very expensive.
Yemekten sonra kahve içmeyelim. Let's not have coffee after dinner (after the meal).

2 The second person is generally not used at all. Instead, the imperative form performs the same function.

3 The third person form with no personal suffix after the optative is not used except in some set expressions. The form with the -SİN suffix, without the optative ending, is regularly used.

Çay açık olsun lütfen. Let the tea be weak, please. (Please make the tea weak.)
Hava biraz soğuk, denize girmesin. It is a little cold, don't let him go in the sea.
Yarın gelmesin. Let him not come tomorrow.
Bahçede oynasınlar. Let them play in the garden.

Some commonly used set expressions:

Geçmiş olsun. Let it pass. (Let it be over: used particularly to someone who is ill.)
Bereket versin. May he (God) grant you plenty.
Allah korusun. May God protect.

The optative is used with the past suffix **-(Y)Dİ** to express regret for something that has not taken place and the wish that it had:

Doğruyu söyleyeydi. I wish he had told the truth.
Zengin olaydım ... I wish I were rich.

74 -Kİ

This is a suffix used when a noun in the locative or genitive case (noun + **DE**/noun + **(N)İN**) is used to qualify another noun. After locatives:

sokaktaki araba the car in the street
oteldeki müşteriler the customers in the hotel
Köşedeki bina bizim otelimiz.
The building on the corner is our hotel.
Plajdaki şemsiyelerin sayısı çok az.
The number of the umbrellas on the beach is very small.

The above forms in **-Kİ** can also stand for the noun if there has been a previous reference to the noun qualified by **-Kİ**:

Lokantadaki müşteriler İngiliz, oteldekiler Alman.
The customers in the restaurant are British, those that are in the hotel are German. (**müşteriler** is in the plural, so we put the plural suffix **-ler** after **oteldeki-**)

After genitives:

otelinki the hotel's, the one which is the hotel's
kuterununki the box's, the one which belongs to the box

When used with the genitive suffix, **-Kİ** stands for the noun rather than describing it. In such cases it is understood that there has been a reference to the noun in question and **-Kİ** saves us repeating it.

Bu lokantanın otoparkı küçük, otelinki büyük. The car park of this restaurant is small, the hotel's (meaning the car park of the hotel) is big.
Dolabın rengi beyaz, kutununki kırmızı. The colour of the cupboard is white, that of the box (the one that is of the box) is red.
Elbisem çok eski, Ayşe'ninki yeni. My dress is very old, Ayşe's is new.

All the pronouns can take **-Kİ** when they are in the genitive:

Dersin bitti, benimki şimdi başlıyor. Your lesson is finished, mine (the one which is mine) is starting now.
Havlularımız burada, sizinkiler nerede? Our towels are here, where are yours?

So can the interrogative **kimin** 'whose':

Benim odam çok küçük, kiminki büyük? My room is very small, whose is big?
Onunki kırmızı, kiminki sarı? Hers is red, whose is yellow?

In all its uses described so far, **-Kİ** is a non-harmonic suffix: it is always **-ki**. However, **-Kİ** can also be added to words with a time reference, and with a few of these, **-Kİ** harmonises and becomes **-kü**:

dünkü gazete yesterday's newspaper
bugünkü haber today's news

Other time-related words that take **-Kİ** are the following: **yarın, geçen gün, öbür gün, önce, sonra, sabah, akşam, gece, öğleden sonra, öğleden önce, hafta, yıl** (these last two have to be specified, e.g. **bu haftaki, geçen yılki**).

When a word with **-Kİ** takes a case suffix there has to be the buffer **-n-** between the **-Kİ** suffix and the case ending:

Bu gazeteyi okudum, ama masadakini okumadım. I read this newspaper, but I did not read the one on the table.
Türkiye'de bu yıl geçen yılkinden daha fazla turist var. There are more tourists in Turkey this year than last year.
Bu ceket senin, benimkinde cep yoktu. This jacket is yours, there were no pockets on mine.

Exercise 20

Translate the following:
1 Please do not smoke.
2 Shut the door please.
3 Let's wait for them.
4 Our suitcases are heavy, so let's go to the hotel by taxi.
5 The books that are on the table are mine.

75 The future tense: -(Y)ECEK

The suffix that indicates future tense is **-(Y)ECEK** (when a vowel
follows it, **k** changes into **ğ**), and it takes the same personal suffixes as
-(İ)YOR. It is used to describe an action that will take place. Its variants
are **-yecek** or **-yacak** when the verb base ends in a vowel, and **-ecek** or
-acak when the verb base ends in a consonant.

Sizi beşe kadar bekleyeceğim. I shall wait for you until five.
Film geç başlayacak. The film will start late.

If **-yecek** or **-yacak** is preceded by the vowels **e** or **a** then these are
pronounced **i** and **ı** respectively in spoken Turkish. This change is
sometimes reflected in informal writing as well.

Yarın arkadaşıma gideceğim. I shall go to my friend's tomorrow.
Anahtarı resepsiyona bırakacaksın. You will leave the key at the
reception.
Beşten sonra gelecek. He will come after five.
Size Çarşambadan önce telefon edeceğiz. We shall ring you before
Wednesday.
Köşedeki mağazada çok iyi kalite deri ceketler bulacaksınız.
You will find very good quality leather jackets in the store on the corner.
Bize yeni kitaplar verecekler. They will give us new books.

76 Questions with -(Y)ECEK

verb + future + question + person

| gel | ecek | mi | siniz? | gelecek misiniz? will you come? |
| oku | yacak | mı | yım? | okuyacak mıyım? shall I read? |

As with the other tenses, the third person plural suffix comes before the
question marker:

Bu yıl tatile gidecekler mi? Will they go on holiday this year?

Remember, when there is an interrogative, the **Mİ** question marker is
not used:

Bu yıl nereye tatile gidecekler? Where will they go on holiday this
year?
Hesabı kim ödeyecek? Who will pay the bill?

77 Negative with -(Y)ECEK

verb + negative + future + person

gel	me	yecek	sin	**gelmeyeceksin** you will not come
yaz	ma	yacak	lar	**yazmayacaklar** they will not write

Bu akşam televizyon seyretmeyeceğiz. We shall not watch TV tonight.
Yeni bir ceket almayacağım. I shall not buy a new jacket.

78 Negative questions with -(Y)ECEK

verb + negative + future + question + person

gel	me	yecek	mi	sin

Gelmeyecek misin? Won't you come?

başla	ma	yacak	mı	yız

Başlamayacak mıyız? Shan't we start?
Bu mektuplara cevap vermeyecek misiniz? Won't you reply to these letters?
Çayına süt koymayacak mı? Won't she put milk in her tea?
Gümrükte bavullara bakmayacaklar mı? Won't they look at (check) the suitcases at customs?

79 The future-past

The future tense can be followed by the past form of 'to be', -(Y)Dİ, forming the compound tense of future-past. This indicates action that was going to be performed or that was to take place in the past (but probably did not happen). This tense form translates 'was/were going to ...'.

Ona telefon edecektim ama vazgeçtim. I was going to ring him up, but I changed by mind (lit. I gave up).
Bana bir kitap verecektiniz, yanınızda mı? You were going to give me a book, have you got it with you?
Saat bire kadar geleceklerdi ama gelmediler. They were due to come by one o'clock, but they did not come.

80 gibi: as, like

Gibi *follows* what is being compared; in English the words 'as' and 'like' come *before* what is being compared.

Kızın gözleri deniz gibi mavi. The girl's eyes are blue like the sea.
Kahve bal gibi tatlı. The coffee is sweet like honey.
Ben de Emel gibi Türküm. I too am Turkish, like Emel.
Onlarınki gibi bir evimiz var. We have a house like theirs.

Pronouns with **gibi** are in the genitive:

Benim gibi konuşun. Speak as I do. (Speak like me.)
Bu yemeği sizin gibi yaptım. I made this dish like you (as you did).
Senin gibi mi çalıştı? Did he work like you?

81 için: for

İçin always *follows* the word it refers to:

Araba için yeni bir radyo alacağım. I shall buy a new radio for the car.
Sinema için biletimiz yok. We do not have tickets for the cinema.
Kardeşim için bir hediye aldım. I bought a present for my brother.

When **için** is used with pronouns, the pronouns (except those with the **-LER** plural suffix) have to be in the genitive:

Bu benim için çok değerli bir armağan. This is a very valuable (precious) present for me.
Bunun fiyatı onlar için çok fazla. The price of this is too much for them.

In most situations **için** can be replaced by the dative **-(Y)E**, but **için** is more easily distinguishable and more emphatic:

Bu palto Ayşe için biraz büyük.
Bu palto Ayşe'ye biraz büyük. } This coat is a little big for Ayşe.
Bu paket kimin için?
Bu paket kime? } Who is this parcel for?

98

82 Derivational suffix: -LİK

This suffix is added to nouns to form adjectives, and to adjectives to form nouns. Its variants are **-lik, -lık, -lük** and **-luk**.

güzel	beautiful	**güzellik**	beauty
iyi	good	**iyilik**	goodness
hasta	sick	**hastalık**	illness
temiz	clean	**temizlik**	cleanliness
kim	who	**kimlik**	identity
gün	day	**günlük**	daily
baş	head	**başlık**	headline

This suffix also means 'for', like the word **için**, so it can sometimes be used interchangeably with **için**:

İki kişilik bir oda istiyorum.
İki kişi için bir oda istiyorum. } I want a room for two.

With the meaning of 'for', the **-LİK** suffix is mostly used as a straightforward adjective:

Üç haftalık bir tatil yaptık. We had a three-week holiday.
İki kişilik bir yatak aldık. We bought a double bed (bed for two).
Günlük gazetelerin başlıklarını okuyor. He reads the headlines of the daily newspapers.

The **-LİK** suffix also indicates the purpose for which something is intended or used:

kitap	book	**kitaplık**	book-case/library
göz	eye	**gözlük**	spectacles
tuz	salt	**tuzluk**	salt-cellar
süt	milk	**sütlük**	milk jug

The **-LİK** suffix can often follow the **-Lİ, -SİZ** and **-Cİ** (see section 98) suffixes, indicating respectively a state of having, not having and being something:

canlı	lively	**canlılık**	liveliness
akılsız	unintelligent/stupid	**akılsızlık**	stupidity
dişçi	dentist	**dişçilik**	dentistry/state of being a dentist

83 hakkında: about, concerning

The word **hakkında** is formed by adding a possessive suffix to the base, which is in turn followed by the suffix **-DE**:

hakkımda	about me
hakkında	about you (sing)
hakkında	about him/her/it
hakkımızda	about us
hakkınızda	about you (pl/formal)
haklarında	about them

Hakkımda size ne sordular? What did they ask you about me?
Bunun hakkında çok şey biliyorsunuz. You know a lot about this.
Arkadaşlarınız hakkında ne düşünüyorsunuz? What do you think of (about) your friends?

Vocabulary

gürültü	noise	**cevap vermek**	to answer
şoför	driver (professional)	**değerli**	valuable
		bal	honey
sarkmak	to lean out	**tatlı**	sweet (adjective), dessert
şemsiye	umbrella		
olmak	to become	**düşünmek**	to think
hazırlamak	to prepare	**vazgeçmek**	to give up
havaalanı	airport	**toplantı**	meeting
köşe	corner	**fabrika**	factory
müşteri	customer	**kurmak**	to set up, establish, found
bina	building		
ders	lesson	**dil**	language, tongue
başlamak	to begin	**diğer**	other
ödemek	to pay	**öteki**	other
mağaza	store, large shop	**sayı**	number
resepsiyon	reception (at a hotel)	**böylece**	thus
		rapor	report
seyretmek	to watch	**süre**	period
gümrük	customs		

READING

Gelecek hafta bir toplantı için Ankara'ya gideceğim. Ankara'da üç gün kaldıktan sonra uçakla İzmir'e geçeceğim. İzmir'de büyük bir fabrika kuruyoruz. Bu fabrika İngiltere'deki fabrikalar gibi olacak. Fabrikadaki işçi sayısı sekiz yüz elli kadar. Bu işçilerden bazılarını üçer aylık bir süre için İngiltere'ye göndereceğiz, böylece biraz İngilizce öğrenecekler. İzmir'de fabrikanın müdürü ve diğer kişilerle konuştuktan sonra Londra'ya döneceğim. Gezim hakkında kısa bir rapor yazacağım.

Exercise 21

Translate the following:
1 I shall buy a new car.
2 Will you (pl) come tomorrow?
3 He will not drink water.

Lesson 9

84 The aorist tense

The aorist tense (for uses see section 88 below) has a number of different forms depending on the verb base to which it is added. The personal suffixes this tense takes are the same as those for -(İ)YOR and -(Y)ECEK, and the order of the other suffixes that go with it is also the same as with these tenses.

1 Verbs ending in a vowel take **-R**:

oku_rum	I read
bekle_rsin	you wait
başla_rlar	they start
anlarız	we understand
iste_r	he wants
topla_rsınız	you collect

2 Verbs ending in a consonant take **-İR** or **-ER**. The rules for this distinction are as follows:

a) Verbs of more than one syllable take the suffix **-İR**; variants are **-ir, -ır, -ür, -ur.**

göster_irim	I show
otur_ursunuz	you sit
çalış_ır	he works
öksür_ürüz	we cough

b) The following one-syllable verbs also take **-İR**:

alır	he takes	**olur**	he becomes
bilir	he knows	**ölür**	he dies
bulur	he finds	**sanır**	he thinks
durur	he stops	**varır**	he arrives
gelir	he comes	**verir**	he gives
görür	he sees	**vurur**	he hits
kalır	he stays		

c) All the other one-syllable verbs take **-ER**; variants are **-er**, **-ar**:

gider	he goes	**açar**	he opens
böler	he divides	**çalar**	he rings
tutar	he holds	**koşar**	he runs

85 Negative of the aorist

The aorist tense suffix used with the negative **-ME** is irregular: it is **-Z** for the second and third persons, and drops out altogether for the first person singular and plural.

gel	me	—	m	**gelmem** I do not come
gel	me	z	sin	**gelmezsin** you do not come
gel	me	z	—	**gelmez** he does not come
gel	me	—	yiz	**gelmeyiz** we do not come
gel	me	z	siniz	**gelmezsiniz** you do not come
gel	me	z	ler	**gelmezler** they do not come

Note that in the first person singular, after the negative **-ME**, the personal suffix is just **-M**.

başlamam	I do not start
çalışmazsın	you do not work
bilmez	he does not know
konuşmayız	we do not speak
gitmezsiniz	you do not go
oynamazlar	they do not play

86 Question form of the aorist

There is no irregularity here, and the same formula as for **-(İ)YOR** and **-(Y)ECEK** applies:

gelir miyim?	do I come?
yer misin?	do you eat?
bilir mi?	does he know?
alır mıyız?	do we buy?
içer misiniz?	do you drink?
isterler mi?	do they want?

87 Negative questions with the aorist

The suffix -Z, which is used to indicate the aorist after the **-ME** negative ending, is used with all persons in negative questions:

gelmez miyim?	don't I come?
gitmez misin?	don't you go?
okumaz mı?	doesn't he read?
görmez miyiz?	don't we see?
hatırlamaz mısınız?	don't you remember?
sevmezler mi?	don't they like?

88 Uses of the aorist

The aorist has several different uses.

1   It is used to express actions done habitually or repeatedly, and also to make statements that are true and valid at all times.

Her sabah altıda kalkarım. I get up at six every morning.
Uçak İstanbul'a üç saatte gider. The plane reaches Istanbul in three hours.
İngilizler bu yemeği bilmez. The British do not know this dish.

In this sense of the aorist, it is possible to replace it with **-(İ)YOR**; in fact in colloquial Turkish **-(İ)YOR** seems to be replacing the aorist quite systematically.

Her sabah iki bardak çay içiyorum. I drink two glasses of tea every morning.
Tren Ankara'ya sekiz saatte gidiyor. The train goes to Ankara in eight hours.

2   Another use of the aorist is to express action done voluntarily, willingly and to indicate a hope to do something.

Bu mektubu öğleye kadar bitiririm. I'll finish this letter by noon.
Hafta sonunda sinemaya gideriz. We'll go to the cinema at the weekend.
Ali sana haber verir. Ali will let you know.

In this sense, the aorist seems to mean the same thing as the future, but there is an important difference: the future is more a statement of fact, indicating that the action mentioned will definitely take place. The aorist on the other hand indicates an intention, a willingness.

Aorist: **Sana telefon ederim.** I'll ring you.
Future: **Sana telefon edeceğim.** I shall ring you.

As it conveys an intention rather than a certainty, the word **belki** 'perhaps' is frequently used with the aorist.

Belki erken gelir. Perhaps he'll come early.
Belki biraz sonra gelirler. Perhaps they'll come a little later.

3   The aorist is often used as a polite request asking for something to be done, or offering something. The question form is then used:

Lütfen başlar mısınız? Would you start please?
Kapıyı kapar mısınız? Would you close the door?
Kahve ister misiniz? Would you like (some) coffee?
Ne içersiniz? What would you like to drink?

89 'as soon as'

The positive and negative forms of the aorist used in immediate succession with the same verb base can be translated as 'as soon as'.

Mektubumu alır almaz cevap yaz. As soon as you receive my letter, write a reply.
İstasyondan çıkar çıkmaz sola dön. Turn left as soon as you leave the station.
Odaya girer girmez sizi gördüm. I saw you as soon as I entered the room.
Sabah kalkar kalkmaz bir kahve içerim. I have a (cup of) coffee as soon as I get up in the morning.
Bu dersi bitirir bitirmez yeni derse başlayacaksınız. As soon as you finish this lesson, you will start the new lesson.

The verb carrying the positive and negative forms of the aorist in this 'as soon as' form does not have a personal suffix to show the doer of that action. If the doer of the action is not the same as the doer (subject) of the main verb, then there is usually a pronoun or a noun to tell us what the subject of the clause is. For example:

Orhan odaya girer girmez çıktım. I left as soon as Orhan entered the room.
Ben biner binmez otobüs kalktı. As soon as I got on, the bus started.

90 'used to', 'would have'

The suffix **-(Y)Dİ** can be added to the aorist. The combined form translates 'used to ...' or 'would have ...':

İstanbul'da her Pazar Topkapı Sarayı'na giderdik. In Istanbul we used to go to the Topkapı Palace every Sunday.
Babam Londra'yı sevmezdi, ama şimdi seviyor. My father used not to like London, but now he likes it.
Konya'ya gitmek isterdim. I should have liked to have gone to Konya.

91 İKEN/-(Y)KEN: while

The suffix **-(Y)KEN** is used to mean 'while'. It can also occur as an independent word by itself, **İKEN**, but is seldom so used. After bases that end in a vowel the ending is **-yken**, and after bases that end in a consonant the ending is **-ken**. It is always non-harmonic. It can be used after nouns, adjectives or after verbs, in which case there must be a tense ending preceding it. The syllable preceding **-(Y)KEN** is always stressed. It can be translated into English as 'when' or '-ing' as well as 'while'.

İstanbul'dayken bütün müzeleri gezdik. We visited all the museums while (we were) in Istanbul.
Hastayken doktora gideriz. We go to the doctor when we are ill.
Çocukken çok futbol oynadım. I played a lot of football when I was a child.
Odamdayken telefon çaldı. The phone rang while I was in my room.

When used with a verb base, the tense suffix that precedes **-(Y)KEN** is mostly the aorist.

Yemeğe gelirken çiçek getirdiler. They brought flowers when they came to dinner.
Türkçe öğrenirken iki ay Türkiye'de kaldım. I stayed in Turkey for two months while (when) I was learning Turkish.
Postaneye giderken bu mektubu da götürür müsünüz lütfen? When you go to the post office will you please take this letter as well?

When **-(Y)KEN** is used following the future ending, the combined form
means 'while/just as intending to do something'; and the second part of
the sentence generally shows that the intention has not been fulfilled:

**Ankara'ya trenle gidecekken son dakikada vazgeçtik, otobüsle
gittik.** While we were due to go to Ankara by train, we changed
our mind at the last minute and went by coach.

The same sentence could be shorter without the explanations:
Ankara'ya trenle gidecekken otobüsle gittik. While we were
intending (due) to go to Ankara by train, we went by coach.
Kapıyı açacakken pencereyi açtı. While intending to open the door,
he opened the window.

Exercise 22

Translate the following:
1   Would you like a cold beer?
2   The bus goes from Izmir to Kuşadası in two hours.
3   I saw it as soon as I entered the museum.
4   We spoke Turkish while in Turkey.
5   He closed the door when (while) he left (went out of) the room.

92 Telling the time

You know that the word **saat** means 'clock', 'watch' or 'hour':

Yeni bir saat aldım. I bought a new watch.
Ankara, İstanbul'dan arabayla altı saat uzakta. Ankara is six
hours away from Istanbul by car.

When the word **saat** follow a numeral it means 'hour': **altı saat** 'six
hours', but when **saat** comes before a numeral, it means 'o'clock': **saat
altı** 'six o'clock'.

Saat bir. It is one o'clock.
Yemek saat birde. Lunch (meal) is at one o'clock.
Dört saat çalıştım. I worked for four hours.
Saat dörtte gel. Come at four o'clock.

Similarly with the interrogative **kaç**:

Kaç saat? How many hours?

Saat kaç? What is the time?

Although the last vowel in **saat** is **a**, when a suffix is added to this word, it always has a front vowel **e** or **i**:

saatler hours/clocks/watches
bir saatte in one hour
saati his watch/her watch/clock etc.

When giving the time in Turkish we talk of '... past the hour' and '... to the hour' as in English. The patterns are as follows:

Past the hour: hour + -(Y)İ + minute + **geçiyor**
 beş + i + on + **geçiyor**
Beşi on geçiyor. (It is) ten past five.

You can use the words **saat** and **dakika** as well, but colloquially these are omitted.

Saat beşi on dakika geçiyor. (lit. The time is ten minutes passing five.) It is ten past five.
Sekizi yirmi beş geçiyor. It is twenty-five past eight.
Onikiyi çeyrek geçiyor. It is a quarter past twelve.

To the hour: hour + -(Y)E+ minute + **var**
 beş + e + on + **var**
Beşe on var. It is ten to five.

Saat beşe on dakika var. (lit.) There are ten minutes to five o'clock.
Dokuza yirmi var. It is twenty to nine.
Yediye çeyrek var. It is a quarter to seven.

For the half hour the word **buçuk** is used after the numeral:

dört buçuk half past four
on buçuk half past ten

However, for 'half past twelve' we say **yarım**, *not* **on iki buçuk**.

Saat yarım. It is half past twelve.

When the time is very close to the half hour (roughly up to five minutes before or after the half hour) the half hour is usually taken as the reference point:
İki buçuğa üç var. It is three minutes to half past two (i.e. 2.27).
On buçuğu dört geçiyor. It is four minutes past half past ten (i.e. 10.34).

A different phrasing is needed to say 'at such and such a time'.

Past the hour: hour + -(Y)İ + minute + **geçe**
                   altı + -yı + beş + geçe
altıyı beş geçe at five past six

Dördü çeyrek geçe buluştuk. We met at a quarter past four.
Yarımı beş geçe telefon çaldı. The phone rang at five past half past twelve (at 12.35).
Salı günü üçü on geçe buraya gelin. Come here on Tuesday at ten past three.

To the hour: hour + -(Y)E + minute + **kala**
                  altı + ya + beş + kala
altıya beş kala at five to six

Sekize on kala evden çıktım. I left home at ten to eight.
Posta sabah dokuza çeyrek kala gelir. The post comes at a quarter to nine in the morning.

A simple way of telling the time is to use the 24-hour clock, as in:

Uçak sekiz yirmide kalkıyor. The plane leaves at eight twenty (morning).
Uçak yirmi yirmide kalkıyor. The plane leaves at twenty twenty (evening).
Saat on dokuz, haberleri veriyoruz. It is nineteen hours, here is the news (lit. we are giving the news).
İki kamyon yirmi bir kırkta çarpıştı. The two lorries collided at twenty-one forty.

Although easy to remember, this way of telling the time is only used in special contexts such as the arrival and departure of aircraft, trains, etc. and during the news on the radio and TV.

Vocabulary

genellikle	generally	**kalabalık**	crowded
başka	other	**gürültülü**	noisy
değişik	different	**ulaşım**	transport
tarihi	historical	**zor**	difficult
tur	tour	**şehir**	town, city
düzenlemek	to arrange	**kent**	town, city
yorulmak	to be or become tired		

Exercise 23

Translate the following:
1 Let us meet at half past twelve.
2 The plane takes off from Dalaman at ten to three: we shall be at the airport at half past one.
3 We went to Ankara by train in eight hours.
4 They did not open our suitcases when (while) we passed through customs.

READING

Tatil için her yıl Türkiye'ye gideriz ve üç hafta kalırız. Genellikle Mayıs sonunda gideriz, ya da Eylül ayında. Yaz aylarında gitmeyiz, çünkü hava çok sıcak oluyor. Her yıl başka bir otelde kalırız, böylece değişik yerler görürüz. Oteller yakındaki tarihi yerlere turlar düzenler. Bu turlarla gidince yorulmadan bir çok yer görürüz. Dönerken bir kaç gün İstanbul'da kalırız. İstanbul değişik bir şehir: kalabalık, gürültülü, ulaşım zor ama ben İstanbul'u çok seviyorum, Avrupa şehirleri gibi değil. İstanbul'da biraz alışveriş yaparız. Arkadaşlarımıza küçük hediyeler alırız. Üç haftalık tatil çok çabuk biter. Taksiyle havaalanına giderken ertesi yılki tatilimizi düşünürüz.

Lesson 10

93 Comparatives

The word **daha** is used to mean 'more' or '-er':

daha güzel	more beautiful
daha yavaş	slower
daha ucuz	cheaper
daha iyi	better

Kahve sevmiyorum, çay daha iyi. I do not like coffee, tea is better.
Bodrum çok kalabalık, Kaş daha güzel. Bodrum is very crowded, Kaş is more attractive.
Daha ucuz bir şey var mı? Is there something cheaper?

When you are comparing two things directly, the suffix **-DEN** is used for the English word 'than':

İstanbul Bodrum'dan daha büyük. Istanbul is bigger than Bodrum.

When the things compared are both present in the sentence, as above, **daha** can be left out:

İstanbul Bodrum'dan büyük.
Odam seninkinden rahat. My room is more comfortable than yours.
Elimdeki kitap masadakinden ağır. The book in my hand is heavier than the one on the table.
Kardeşim benden uzun. My sister is taller than I.
Ben kardeşimden şişmanım. I am fatter than my sister.

There can also be various combinations of **daha** with **biraz, az, çok** and **fazla**:

Biraz daha şarap ister misiniz? Would you like a little more wine?
Bugün daha az yoruldum. I am (got) less tired today.
Yarın daha çok para kazanacağım. I shall earn (win) more money tomorrow.
Bu otel çok daha pahalı. This hotel is much more expensive.
Bu yıl Türkiye'de iki hafta kaldık, gelecek yıl biraz daha çok

kalacağız. This year we stayed in Turkey for two weeks, next year we shall stay slightly longer (lit. a little more). **Daha fazla et istemiyorum.** I do not want more meat.

94 Superlatives

Superlatives are formed with **en** 'most', '-est':

en güzel most beautiful
en iyi best
en geniş widest
en soğuk coldest

En güzel elbise benim elbisem. The most beautiful dress is my dress.
Türkiye'de en sıcak ay Temmuzdur. The hottest month in Turkey is July.

For 'the most ... of ...' constructions the genitive or the locative may be used:

Bu evin en büyük odası yemek odası. The largest room of this house is the dining room.
Bu evde en büyük oda yemek odası. In this house the largest room is the dining room.
Dünyanın en zengin adamı kimdir? Who is the richest man in the world?
Mağazadaki en pahalı oyuncağı aldım. I bought the most expensive toy in the store.
Meyvelerden en çok şeftaliyi seviyorum. Among (lit. Of) fruit, I like peaches best (lit. most).
Bu dairede kim en çok çalışıyor? Who works the most in this office?
Bu antika vazo için en az yüz otuz bin lira veririm. I would give at least one hundred and thirty thousand lira for this antique vase.
En çok üç gün tatilimiz var. We have three days holiday at the most.
Yolculuğumuz en az üç buçuk saat sürer. Our journey takes at least three and a half hours.
Bu otelde en fazla dört gece kalacağız. We shall stay four nights at the most in this hotel.

95 Uses of 'daha'

a) 'more'
   Bir gazete daha aldım. I bought one more newspaper.
   İki orta kahve daha lütfen. Two more medium sweet coffees, please.
b) 'more' - comparative
   Türkçe daha zor bir dil. Turkish is a more difficult language.
c) 'still'
   Çok yorgun, daha uyuyor. He is very tired, he is still sleeping.
d) 'yet' - with negatives
   Yeni evinizi daha görmedik. We have not seen your new house yet.
   Daha gelmediler. They have not arrived yet.
e) 'again' - as **bir daha** (once more)
   Bir daha tekrarlayın lütfen. Repeat (it) again please.
   Onunla bir daha konuşmadım. I did not speak to him again.
   Aynı numarayı bir daha çevirin. Dial the same number once more.

96 The reported past: -MİŞ

The suffix that indicates reported past is **-MİŞ**; its variants are **-miş**, **-mış, -müş,** and **-muş.** It is used to report past action that the speaker has not witnessed, but has got to know through an intermediary which is not necessarily a person. In the sense of being past, it is not very different from **-Dİ** past, but unlike **-Dİ**, it has no element of personal experience: the speaker has not personally witnessed the action being described. For this reason it may be translated using expressions like 'apparently', 'so it is said', 'so I understand', etc. The negative, question and negative question forms of **-MİŞ** follow the same pattern as those of **-(İ)YOR** and **-(Y)ECEK.**

Sabahleyin geç kalkmış, onun için işe geç kalmış. He apparently got up late in the morning, and for that reason was, so I understand, late for work.
Bu yaz tatil yapmamışlar. They apparently did not have a holiday this summer.
Ödevinizi yapmamışsınız. I understand that you did not do your homework. (The implication is 'I have just found out that you did not ...')

113

Televizyon seyrederken uyumuşum. I fell asleep while watching TV (so I realise).
Buraya gelirken kimseye haber vermemiş. When coming here, he apparently did not let anyone know.
Kapıyı çalmış ama duymamışım. He apparently did knock on the door, but (apparently) I did not hear it.
Parayı almış mı? Has he got the money?
Yemekleri doğru seçmiş miyiz? Have we selected the dishes correctly?

An element of surprise is often expressed in negative questions with **-MİŞ** (both in questions with **Mİ** and with the interrogatives), and the context would help us to identify this.

Bunu ona söylememiş misiniz? Haven't you told them this?
Bunu nasıl görmemişim? How on earth did I not see this?

The suffix **-(Y)Dİ** can be added to **-MİŞ** to form a compound tense, the past perfect. This compound tense form does not indicate that the action is reported.

Bu filmi daha önce görmüştük. We had seen this film before.
Türkiye'ye gitmemiş miydiniz? Hadn't you been to Turkey?
Dünkü gazeteyi okumamıştı, onun için benimkini verdim. He hadn't read yesterday's paper, so I gave him mine.

Vocabulary

şarap	wine	**ödev**	homework
kazanmak	to win	**mesaj**	message
et	meat	**haber vermek**	to inform, let
şeftali	peach		someone know
daire	office, flat	**çalmak**	to ring, steal, play
çalışmak	to work		(an instrument)
antika	antique	**kapıyı çalmak**	to ring the bell,
vazo	vase		knock on the
tekrarlamak	to repeat		door
tercüme etmek	to translate	**seçmek**	to choose
çevirmek	to translate,	**doğru**	correct(ly)
	dial, turn	**müze**	museum

Exercise 24

Translate the following:

1 The most expensive hotel is not the best hotel.
2 Istanbul is warmer than London.
3 Our room is the smallest in the hotel.
4 The plane apparently arrived very late.
5 I had gone to Istanbul two years previously (before), but I had not seen this museum.

97 İMİŞ/-(Y)MİŞ: reported form of 'to be'

İMİŞ, like **İDİ**, is generally used not as a word by itself but as a suffix: **-(Y)MİŞ**. After bases that end in a vowel its variants are **-ymiş, -ymış, -ymüş** or **-ymuş**, and after bases that end in a consonant they are **-miş, -mış, -müş** and **-muş**. It is followed by the same personal endings as **-MİŞ**. It has no exact time reference; it merely indicates that the speaker has no first-hand information about the statement he is making, but is just reporting what he has either been told or found out. It can also express surprise.

Apart from their grammatical function, the main difference between **-MİŞ** (the reported past suffix which is always added to verb bases) and **İMİŞ** is that, while **-MİŞ** is a past tense (see section 96), **İMİŞ** is timeless. Both share the feature of being used in reporting statements or actions not witnessed. For this reason, in translating into English, words like 'apparently', 'seemingly' or 'supposedly' can be used. Here are some sentences with **İMİŞ** used, as it normally is, as a suffix: **-(Y)MİŞ**.

Çok hastaymış, onun için gelmeyecek. Apparently he is very ill, so he will not come.

Compare the above sentence with:

Çok hasta, onun için gelmeyecek. He is very ill, so he will not come.

In both of the sentences the time reference is the same, the present. The difference is that in the first sentence the information is based on hearsay, not first-hand experience.

Ayşe'nin annesi ve babası İngiltere'deymiş. Ayşe's mother and father are apparently in England.

In negative sentences **-(Y)MİŞ** is added to **değil** and **yok**:

Cevabım yanlış değilmiş. My answer is/was apparently not wrong.
Çocukken yaramaz değilmişim. Apparently when I was a child I
was not naughty. (meaning I was too young to remember it myself, so
I have been told about it)

With the third person plural suffix, **-(Y)MİŞ** is often placed before
-LER, but it is also possible to place it after **-LER**, and this use is
becoming widespread.

Zenginmişler./Zenginlermiş. They are (apparently) rich.
Zengin değilmişler./Zengin değillermiş. They are (apparently) not
rich.

As mentioned above **-(Y)MİŞ** can also express surprise:

Çok yorulmuşum! How tired I am!
Burası ne kadar güzelmiş! How beautiful this place is!
Akıllıymışsın! You *are* clever!

In questions **-(Y)MİŞ** is added to the question marker **Mİ**:

Büyük müymüş? Is it supposed to be big?
Evde miymişiz? Were we (supposedly) at home?
Evde değil miymişiz? Were we supposedly not at home?
Yalnız mıymışsın? Were you supposedly by yourself?

-(Y)MİŞ can also be added to interrogatives:

Kimmiş? Who is it (supposedly)?
Neredeymiş? Where is he (supposedly)?
Neymiş? What is it supposed to be?

-(Y)MİŞ is also used after 'verb + tense' combinations. In such
instances the tense suffix following the verb gives the time of the action
and **-(Y)MİŞ** does not change that time reference at all. It only conveys
the sense of 'apparently', 'supposedly', etc.

Ayşe Londra'ya gidiyormuş. Ayşe, apparently, is going to London.
Otelin yeni lokantası yarın açılacakmış. The hotel's new
restaurant will (apparently) open tomorrow.
Her sabah altıda kalkarmış. He (apparently) gets up at six every
morning.

Although grammatically possible, **-(Y)MİŞ** is seldom used after the tense suffixes **-Dİ** and **-MİŞ**, and you would not have any occasion to use such combinations.

98 Derivational suffixes: -Cİ and -(Y)İCİ

-Cİ

This suffix is added to nouns to form other nouns indicating the occupation, association or belief of a person. It has eight possible variants: **-çi, -çı, -çü, -çu** after voiceless consonants and **-ci, -cı, -cü, -cu** after all other sounds.

süt	milk	**sütçü**	milkman
yol	road	**yolcu**	traveller, passenger

sözcü	spokesman
kapıcı	doorman, caretaker
dişçi	dentist
yalancı	liar
milliyetçi	nationalist
sağcı	right-winger (politics)
solcu	left-winger (politics)
halkçı	populist (politics)

-(Y)İCİ

This suffix has the same function as **-Cİ** above, but it is only added to verbs. It indicates a person or a quality, and thus forms adjectives as well as nouns.

dinleyici	listener
satıcı	seller
alıcı	buyer
okuyucu	reader

besleyici	nourishing
üzücü	saddening
yorucu	tiring

Exercise 25

Translate the following:

1 Apparently the weather is very cold in Antalya.
2 I rang Ayşe, but apparently she was not at home.
3 He will apparently stay there two weeks.
4 Milk is supposed to be very nourishing.
5 The passengers had apparently been waiting for the plane for three hours.

Vocabulary

şimdilik	for the moment
maalesef	unfortunately
taraf	side
deniz tarafı	the side overlooking the sea (lit. the sea side)
bahçe tarafı	the side overlooking the garden (lit. the garden side)
giriş	entry, entrance
giriş yolu	approach road
Katma Değer Vergisi (KDV)	Value Added Tax (VAT)
dahil	included
hariç	not included, extra
pasaport	passport
kimlik	identity

CONVERSATION

Resepsiyonda

– İyi günler.
– İyi günler. Buyurun efendim.
– Boş odanız var mı?
– Bu akşam için mi?
– Evet.
– Kaç kişilik bir oda?
– İki kişilik lütfen.
– Kaç gün kalacaksınız?
– Şimdilik üç gün.

- Üç gece için odamız yok, maalesef, ancak iki gece için banyolu ve güzel bir odamız var. Üçüncü gece için size başka bir oda verelim.
- Bu odalar deniz tarafında mı?
- Birinci oda bahçe tarafında, ikinci oda denize bakıyor.
- Bahçe tarafı gürültülü mü?
- Hayır, bahçemiz çok büyük, otelin giriş yolu binadan uzakta. Bahçeye bakan odalarımız daha ucuz.
- Gecesi ne kadar?
- İki kişi doksan bin lira. Deniz tarafındaki odanın gecesi yüz on bin lira. Buna KDV (Katma Değer Vergisi) dahil.
- Kahvaltı dahil mi?
- Hayır, kahvaltı hariç. Kahvaltı bir kişi için iki bin beş yüz lira.
- Peki, üç gün burada kalalım.
- Pasaportunuzu veya kimliğinizi verir misiniz?
- Buyurun.
- Teşekkürler.

Lesson 11

99 ya ... ya ... : either ... or ...

The most common form of 'either ... or ...' construction in Turkish is **ya ... ya ...** or **ya ... ya da ...**:

Boş zamanlarımda ya kitap okurum, ya mektup yazarım.
In my free time I either read books or write letters.
İstanbul'da ya dört gün kalırız ya beş gün.
We shall stay in Istanbul either for four or for five days.
Bu kitabı bana ya Ahmet ya da Mehmet verdi.
Either Ahmet or Mehmet gave me this book.

Another possible combination which functions similarly is **ya ... yahut da ...**, but this is less frequently used than the above forms.

Temmuz'un ya altısında yahut da onaltısında dönecekler.
They will come back either on the 6th July or on the 16th.

100 ne ... ne ... : neither ... nor ...

For 'neither ... nor ...', the form to use is **ne ... ne ...**, or **ne ... ne de ...** The negatives **-ME** or **değil** cannot be used with this form.

Otel çok rahat, ne kalabalık, ne gürültülü.
The hotel is very comfortable, it is neither crowded nor noisy.
Tatilde ne müzelere gittik, ne de alışverişe; yalnız denize girdik.
During the holiday we went neither to the museums nor shopping; we just went in the sea.
Yemekte ne et yedi, ne şarap içti.
He neither ate meat nor drank wine at dinner.

101 hem ... hem ... : both ... and ...

Used singly, **hem** comes at the beginning of a sentence or clause, and means 'and, yet, also' depending on the context. It can also be used with **de** as **hem de**, which has the same meanings but is more emphatic. In both uses, **hem** establishes a link or a reference to a previous statement.

Hem ben size söyledim, bu yanlış. And I told you, this is wrong.

In the symmetrically repeated form, **hem ... hem ...** means 'both ... and ...':

Hem çok çalışkan hem çok akıllı.
He is both very hard-working and very clever.

Hafta sonunda hem diskoya gittik hem de sinemaya.
At the weekend we went both to the disco and also to the cinema.

Hem televizyon seyrettim hem kitap okudum.
I both watched TV and read a book.

102 gerek ... gerek ... : both ... and ...

As a single word **gerek** means 'necessary'; but repeated symmetrically **gerek ... gerek ...** generally has the same function and meaning as **hem ... hem ...**; it often accompanies nouns and adjectives and is less frequently used than **hem ... hem ...**

Gerek Marmaris gerek Bodrum yazın çok kalabalıktır.
Both Marmaris and Bodrum are very crowded in the summer.

103 when: -(Y)İNCE

This suffix is added to verbs and indicates consecutive action between two verbs: the action of the verb carrying the **-(Y)İNCE** suffix immediately precedes that of the main verb. It subordinates one sentence to the other. Its variants are: **-yince, -yınca, -yünce, -yunca** after vowels, and **-ince, -ınca, -ünce, -unca** after consonants. It does not have tense or person endings: person is indicated by a pronoun or a subject word, and the tense it conveys is dependent on the main verb.

Ben derse gelince öğretmenimi gördüm.
When I came to the lesson, I saw my teacher.

This sentence can be said without the pronoun **ben**, as the person doing the action is the same for both parts of the sentence:

Derse gelince öğretmenimi gördüm.
Çok konuşunca yoruluyoruz. When we talk a lot, we get tired.

Haberler başlayınca televizyonun sesini açtım.
When the news began, I turned on the sound of the TV. (In the first
part of the sentence the subject is 'the news', in the second part of the
sentence the subject is 'I', so the verb takes the first person ending,
açtı̲m.)
Akşam erken yatınca sabah erken kalkıyorum.
When I go to bed early in the evening, I get up early in the morning.
Siz telefon etmeyince sinemaya gitmedik.
When you did not ring, we did not go to the cinema.

If there is no verb to take the **-(Y)İNCE** suffix, then the verb **ol-** is
used. For example:

Ben hasta olunca annem doktor çağırıyor.
When I am (I become) ill, my mother calls a doctor.
Hava güzel olunca pikniğe gidiyoruz.
When the weather is nice, we go for a picnic.
İşin olmayınca ne yapıyorsun?
What do you do when you have no work?

104 by ...ing, -ing: -(Y)EREK

This suffix, which is added to verbs, indicates action simultaneous with
the main verb of the sentence. The two actions can also be in immediate
sequence. Its variants are **-yerek** and **-yarak** after verbs ending in a
vowel, and **-erek** and **-arak** after verbs ending in a consonant.

Arkadaşından mektup alarak sevindi.
Receiving a letter from his friend, he was pleased.
Bankadan para alarak alışverişe gittim.
Taking money from the bank, I went shopping.

-(Y)EREK also indicates the manner of doing something:

Haberi alınca koşarak geldim. When I got the news, I came running.
Hırsız arka kapıyı açarak içeri girdi. The thief got in by opening
the back door.
İstasyona yürüyerek gittim. I went to the station on foot (lit. by
walking).
Garsonu çağırarak hesabı istedi. Calling the waiter, he asked for
the bill.
Bir şey söylemeyerek çıktı. He left (went out) not saying anything
(without saying anything).

122

Bu yıl tatile gitmeyerek para biriktireceğim. This year, by not going on holiday I'll save (some) money.

The verb **ol-** takes on a special meaning when used with this suffix: **olarak**, and although it literally translates 'being', it generally means 'as'.

Türkiye'de turist olarak dört ay kaldım. I stayed in Turkey for four months as a tourist.

Tatlı olarak ne var? What is there as dessert?

Arkadaş olarak kalalım. Let's stay (as) friends.

Bu sorunun cevabını tam olarak bilmiyorum. I do not know the answer to this question exactly (as a whole).

105 -ing: -(Y)E

The suffix **-(Y)E** added to verb bases is rather similar to **-(Y)EREK**: it generally refers to the manner in which an action is performed, but the essential function of this ending is to indicate that the action is repeated and continuous. Its variants are **-ye, -ya** after vowels and **-e, -a** after consonants. The verb that takes the **-(Y)E** suffix is always repeated.

Sokak çok gürültülü, onun için bağıra bağıra konuşuyor. The street is very noisy, so he is talking shouting (i.e. in a loud voice).

Haberi alınca koşa koşa geldim. I came running when I got the news.

Numaralara baka baka evi bulduk. Looking at the numbers we found the house.

Kitap okuya okuya gözlerim yoruldu. My eyes got tired (through constantly) reading books.

Often the repeated verb with the **-(Y)E** suffix is best translated as a single adverb.

Bu işi seve seve yaparım. I would do this task willingly.

Partiye istemeye istemeye gidiyorum. I am going to the party unwillingly.

The expression we use when seeing people off, **güle güle**, is an example of this structure, meaning 'go happily' (literally: laughing laughing/laughingly).

It is possible to have structures where the verb with the **-(Y)E** suffix is not repeated, but is then followed by another verb. The most frequently used of these are **kalmak** and **durmak**, and they indicate that the action referred to by the verb carrying the **-(Y)E** suffix is repeatedly or constantly done.

Sen kitabını okuya dur, ben çay yaparım.
You keep on reading your book, I'll make the tea.
Çok şaşırdım, adamın yüzüne bakakaldım.
I was very surprised, I kept staring at the man's face.

106 without: -MEDEN

This suffix combination means 'without ...ing'; that is, without a certain action being done. Its variants are **-meden** or **-madan**.

Para almadan alış verişe çıkmış.
He (apparently) went shopping without taking any money.
Kitabı okumadan geri verdi.
He gave the book back without reading (it).
Sorusunu anlamadan cevaplamaya çalıştım.
I tried to answer his question without understanding it.
Durmadan çalışıyor. He is working without stopping (continually).
Sabahtan beri durmadan konuşuyorum.
I have been talking ever since the morning (lit. without stopping).

Another suffix combination which also means 'without' is **-MEKSİZİN**, but this is now rarely used and **-MEDEN** is the preferred form.

107 since: -(Y)ELİ

There are a number of ways of saying 'since' and **-(Y)ELİ** is less frequent than the others. Its variants are **-yeli, -yalı** after vowels, and **-eli, -alı** after consonants.

Ders başlayalı yarım saat oldu.
It has been half an hour since the lesson started.

This suffix also exists in the forms **-(Y)ELİ BERİ** and **-(Y)ELİDEN BERİ**; they are not frequently used either.

124

108 and: -(Y)İP

This suffix does not have a directly translatable meaning: its function is to join two sentences where both verbs have the same tense and person suffix. Consider the following two sentences:

Bu hafta sonu kitap okuyacağım. Bu hafta sonu mektup yazacağım.
I shall read books this weekend. I shall write letters this weekend.

These two sentences could be joined by **ve** 'and', thus saving us the repetition of 'this weekend':

Bu hafta sonu kitap okuyacağım ve mektup yazacağım.
This weekend I shall read books and I shall write letters.

We can now take this shortening a stage further and replace the word **ve** with **-(Y)İP**, by adding it on to the first verb, which becomes the subordinate verb; this subordinate verb does not take any tense or person suffixes, but just **-(Y)İP**, and the tense and person suffixes of the main verb stand for the tense and person of the subordinate verb carrying **-(Y)İP**:

Bu hafta sonu kitap okuyup mektup yazacağım.
This weekend I shall read books and write letters.
Doktora telefon edip randevu alacağım.
I shall ring the doctor and make (lit. take) an appointment.

When the verb is in the negative, **-(Y)İP** can be translated as 'but':

Plaja gitmeyip müzeye gideceğiz.
We shall not go to the beach (but) we shall go to the museum.
Uçağa binmeyip trenle gideceğiz.
We shall not get on a plane (but) we shall go by train.

-(Y)İP is also used in 'whether or not' constructions. These are formed by using the same verb twice, first with the **-(Y)İP** ending and then immediately afterwards with the **-ME** negative suffix followed by the appropriate verbal noun/participle and personal suffixes. This is explained later and examples are given in section 131.

109 rather than: -MEKTENSE

This suffix combination is used to indicate preference. Its variants are

-mektense and **-maktansa**.

Havuza girmektense plaja gidelim.
Rather than going in the pool, let's go to the beach.
Mektup yazmaktansa telefon etmeyi tercih ediyor.
Rather than writing a letter, he prefers to ring up.

110 as, whenever, the more: -DİKÇE

This suffix combination refers to action not done continuously but repeated at various intervals. The initial consonant of the suffix, **d**, becomes **t** after voiceless consonants, and the rest of the suffix harmonises with the base as usual.

İstasyona yaklaştıkça koşmaya başladı.
He started running as he approached the station.
Buna baktıkça beni hatırlarsınız.
Whenever you look at this, you will remember me.
Bu yemeği yedikçe yemek istiyorum.
The more I eat this dish, the more I want to eat it.

Two words with this suffix combination have acquired special meanings:

gittikçe   gradually
oldukça   rather, quite, somewhat

Exercise 26

Translate the following:
1 I drink neither tea nor coffee; I like fruit juice.
2 The garden of his house is both large and sunny.
3 When you open the window, close the door please.
4 Putting on our bathing suits, we went to the beach.
5 You (pl) will stay at home and wait for us.
6 I got tired (through constantly) working all day.
7 They left (went) without waiting for us.
8 I haven't seen him since he arrived here.
9 Rather than sitting in the sun, let's go in the sea.
10 Whenever I look at these pictures, I become happy.

Lesson 12

111 Verbal nouns

Certain suffixes which are added to verbs cause these verbs to function like nouns in the sentence; their grammatical function is the same as any noun, and they are discussed in sections 112 to 114 below.

112 -MEK: the infinitive

We have already seen that the suffix -MEK (variants are -mek and -mak) is often used when listing verbs in a dictionary:

yemek	to eat	açmak	to open
gitmek	to go	kırmak	to brake
yüzmek	to swim	okumak	to read
görmek	to see	koşmak	to run

This ending can also be translated as '-ing'. As verbal nouns, forms with -MEK are used to imply the action of a given verb. The infinitive, i.e. -MEK form, never takes the possessive or the genitive suffixes.

The infinitive can be the subject of the sentence:

Sigara içmek sağlığa zararlıdır. Smoking is harmful to health.
Burada park etmek yasaktır. Parking here is forbidden.

It can be the object. When the infinitive is the object of the verb **istemek** in a sentence, the object ending -(Y)İ is generally omitted.

Yaşamak istiyorum. I want to live.
Bu yaz nereye gitmek istiyorsunuz? Where do you want to go this summer?
Bugün sokağa çıkmak istemedi. She did not want to go out today.

When -MEK is followed by the definite object (accusative) suffix, the final k in -MEK becomes ğ (in fact, whenever a vowel comes after -MEK, this k to ğ change will take place):

Arkadaşıma doğum günü için güzel bir hediye almağı düşünüyorum.
I am thinking of buying a nice present for my friend for her birthday.
Sabahları kahvaltıdan önce deniz kıyısında yürümeği çok seviyorum.
I very much like walking along the sea shore in the mornings before breakfast.

In present-day Turkish, the combination **-MEK** + definite object suffix **-(Y)İ**, that is **-meği/-mağı**, is replaced by **-meyi/-mayı**. This does not affect the meaning and is quite a common process in the language. (See the short infinitive **-ME** below.)

Bizimle gelı ıeği kabul etti. ⎫
Bizimle gelmeyi kabul etti. ⎭ He agreed to come with us.

Verbal nouns with **-MEK** can be the qualifier in a possessive compound:

görüşmek umudu a hope to see (or: hope of seeing)
buluşmak dileği a wish to meet
ölmek zamanı time to die (or: time for dying)

-MEK + **için** means 'in order to':

Paketi göndermek için postaneye gittim.
I went to the post office in order to post (send) the parcel.
Arkadaşlarımı görmek için Ankara'ya gidiyorum.
I am going to Ankara in order to see my friends.

-MEK + **üzere** has a similar meaning of purpose or intention:

Sorularımızı cevaplamak üzere bir basın toplantısı düzenledi.
He arranged a press conference (in order to) answer our questions.
Gürüşmek üzere. Be seeing you. (phrase used for 'goodbye')

-MEK + **üzere** can also mean 'just about to (do something)':

Telefon çaldı, fakat ben çıkmak üzereydim onun için açmadım.
The telephone rang, but I was just about to go out so I did not answer.
Biraz bekler misiniz lütfen, işim bitmek üzere.
Could you wait a little while please, my task is just about to end (I am just about to finish).

-MEK + -(Y)E

Notice the **k** becoming **ğ** before the dative ending **-e** or **-a**.

Yağmur yağmağa başladı. It started to rain. **Bu mektubu yarım saate kadar bitirmeğe çalışıyorum.** I am trying to finish this letter in half an hour.

-MEK + -DE

Böyle söylemekte haklısın. You are right in saying so. **Aynı konuyu sürekli konuşmakta yarar yok.** There is no point in continually discussing the same topic.

-MEK + -DEN

Çalışmaktan kimseye zarar gelmez. No harm comes to anyone from working hard. (Hard work does not harm anyone.) **Her yıl aynı yere gitmekten bıktım.** I am fed up with going to the same place every year.

113 -ME: short infinitive

The verbal noun suffix **-ME** is often referred to as the short infinitive. It is interchangeable with **-MEK** in most situations. **-ME** takes all the case suffixes and the possessive suffix, while **-MEK** does not take the genitive or the possessive suffix. The variants of **-ME** are **-me** and **-ma**. In form it is like the negative suffix **-ME**, but the stress is different: the negative **-ME** throws the stress on the syllable preceding it, e.g. **yázma** 'do not write', but the short infinitive **-ME** carries the stress itself: **yazmá** 'manuscript'.

Verbal nouns with **-ME** occur in compounds like:

okuma haftası	reading week
oturma odası	living room
bekleme odası	waiting room
çalışma saatleri	working hours

-ME is productive in forming common nouns:

konuşma	speech
asma	vine
dolma	dish made by stuffing
	peppers or vine-leaves
dondurma	ice-cream

Forms with **-ME** are often used as adjectives as well:

dolma kalem	fountain pen
asma kat	mezzanine floor
yapma çiçek	artificial flowers
çekme yatak	pull-out bed

-ME takes the possessive (unlike **-MEK**):

Ayşe'nin bu oteli seçmesi bizim için iyi oldu. Ayşe's choosing this hotel has been good (a good thing) for us.
Bu makinayı kullanmasını bilmiyorum. I do not know the using of this machine. (i.e. I do not know how to use this machine.)
Bu kadar geç gelmenizin sebebi nedir? What is the cause of your coming so late? (i.e. Why are you so late?)
Saat on ikiye kadar odayı boşaltmamızı istediler. They wanted our vacating the room by 12 o'clock. (They asked us to vacate the room...)

-ME is also used for putting commands into indirect speech; a direct imperative is not used, but the imperative/command is included in another sentence as the object of verbs like **söylemek** 'tell', **rica etmek** 'request/ask', **emretmek** 'order/command':

Arkadaşıma hafta sonunda gelmesini rica ettim. I asked my friend to come at the weekend.
Turizm Bakanı kıyıdaki gazinoları kaldırmalarını emretti. The Minister for Tourism ordered them to remove the cafés on the shore. (lit. The Minister for Tourism ordered their removing the cafés...)

-ME + possessive can also be used with **için** meaning 'in order to' like **-MEK** + **için**, but here the possessive ending states the person:

İlaçlarını almam için eczaneye gitmemi istedi. He asked me to go to the chemist for my buying his medicines (... so I could buy ...)

İlaçlarını __almak için__ eczaneye gitmemi istedi. He asked me to go to the chemist in order to buy his medicines. (The person who is to do the buying is not specified; we only assume that it is 'I' because of __gitmemi__.)

-ME + possessive + -(Y)E rağmen: although, despite

The short infinitive __-ME__ + possessive can take __-(Y)E rağmen__ meaning 'although, despite, in spite of'.

__Çok çalışmama rağmen az para kazanıyorum.__ (lit. Despite my working hard I earn little money.) Although I work hard, I earn little.
__Bizi uyarmalarına rağmen onları dinlemedik.__ (lit. Despite their warning us, we did not listen to them.) Although they warned us, we did not take any notice.
__Çikolatayı çok sevmesine rağmen yemiyor, çünkü rejimde.__ (lit. Despite her liking chocolates very much, she is not eating, because she is on a diet.) Although she loves chocolates, she does not eat any because she is on a diet.

__-(Y)E rağmen__ can be added to pronouns:

__Beş dilim ekmek yedim, buna rağmen doymadım.__ I ate five slices of bread, despite this I am not full.
__Sen bana karşı oynadın, ama sana rağmen maçı kazandım.__
You played against me, but in spite of you I won the match.

Exercise 27

Translate the following:
1 I do not want to stay here.
2 Where did you go to buy stamps?
3 He will try to ring us before five.
4 We asked him to be at the hotel.
5 Although you told me this, I did not understand it.

114 -(Y)İŞ

The verbal noun suffix __-(Y)İŞ__ refers to the manner of doing something, performing an action. Words formed with __-(Y)İŞ__ can also be established nouns. For example, from the verb __yürümek__ 'to walk' we have

yürüyüş which means:
a) the manner of walking
   Bu kız çok güzel ama yürüyüşü çok tuhaf. This girl is very
   beautiful, but the way she walks (the manner of her walking) is
   very strange.
b) a walk
   Çok uzun bir yürüyüşten sonra otelimize döndük. We
   returned to our hotel after a very long walk.

Some nouns with **-(Y)IŞ:**

alışveriş	shopping
giriş	entrance
çıkış	exit
buluş	invention

Müzenin girişi nerede? Where is the museum('s) entrance?
İşten çıkış saatinde yollar çok kalabalık. The roads are very
crowded at the hour of leaving work (rush hour).

115 lazım: necessary

The word **lazım** indicates a necessity or a need. The thing or action
that is necessary or needed becomes the subject of **lazım**. Verbal nouns
in **-MEK** and **-ME** are often the subject of **lazım:**

Bunu anlamak için biraz daha okuman lazım. You have to read
a little more in order to understand this. (lit. Your reading this a little
more is necessary in order for you to understand this.)
Bu sabah ona kadar İstanbul'a telefon etmem lazım. I have to
ring up Istanbul by ten this morning. (My ringing up Istanbul is
necessary...)
Bu hafta sonu gitmeniz lazım mı? Do you have to go this weekend?
(Is your going this weekend necessary?)

Used in this form **lazım** can also mean 'should':

Bu saatte işte olması lazım. He should be at work at this hour.
Bunu bilmemiz lazım. We should know this.

When **lazım** indicates a need for something, the thing or person in
need takes the dative suffix **-(Y)E:**

Arabaya benzin lazım. The car needs petrol. (Petrol is needed to/for the car.)
Otele müşteri lazım. The hotel needs customers. (Customers are needed to/for the hotel.)
Bana yeni bir elbise lazım. I need a new dress.
Sana para lazım mı? Do you need any money?
Sana bunu almak için kaç para lazım? How much money do you need to buy this?

In negative constructions with **lazım, değil** is put after **lazım**:

Bu kitabı okumanız lazım değil. You do not have to read this book. (lit. Your reading this book is not necessary.)
Mutlu olmak için para lazım değil. You do not need money to be happy. (lit. Money is not needed for to be happy.)

When **lazım** follows the negative of the verbal noun, it indicates a need *not* to do something:

Bu kitabı okumamanız lazım. You must not read this book. (lit. Your not reading this book is necessary.)

The verb **gerekmek** is also frequently used to replace **lazım**:

Saat birde otelde olmam gerekiyor. I have to be at the hotel at one o'clock.
Hastaneye kadar benimle gelmeniz gerekmez. It is not necessary for you to come to the hospital with me.
Otele on beş gün için kaç para ödememiz gerekecek? How much shall we have to pay for the hotel for fifteen days?
Kaç gün daha kalmanız gerek? How many more days must you stay?
Bunu hemen bitirmem gerekmiyor. I do not have to finish this at once.

There are three compound verbs which indicate a need and a necessity:
lazım olmak   to become (be) needed
lazım gelmek   to become (be) necessary
lüzum görmek   to find something necessary.

Lazım olmak implies an object becoming needed for a task:

Tatile giderken sivrisinek ilacı götürdüm, ama lazım olmadı.
When going on holiday I took something for mosquitos (lit. mosquito medicine), but it was not needed.

Şemsiyeni yanına al, belki lazım olur. Take your umbrella with you, you may need it (lit. perhaps it will become needed).

Lazım gelmek implies that doing a certain action has or will become necessary.

Onu görünce konuşmam lazım gelecek. I shall have to speak (to him) when I see him. (lit. My speaking will be/become necessary when I see him.)
Bunun hepsini bitirmeniz lazım gelmez. You don't have to finish all of this. (lit. Your finishing all of this will not be/become necessary.)

Lüzum görmek requires a dative suffix, **-(Y)E**, before it, and is used to imply that one finds something necessary.

Sizin gelmenize lüzum görünce haber veririm. When I find (consider) your coming necessary, I'll let you know.
Doktor hastaneye gitmeme lüzum görmedi. The doctor did not think I should go to the hospital. (lit. The doctor did not find my going to the hospital necessary.)

You don't have to use these forms yourself, because speaking in simple Turkish **lazım** and **gerek** will serve your needs, but you may hear these around you or see them in print.

The words **lüzum** and **gerek** are both used to mean 'necessity'. **Lüzumsuz** or **gereksiz** mean 'unnecessary', and **lüzum yok** or **gerek yok** mean 'there is no need'.

116 -MELİ: the necessitative

The necessity of having to do something can also be expressed by adding the suffix **-MELİ** to verbs: verb + (negative) + **MELİ** + person. Its different forms are **-meli** and **malı**.

gelmeliyim	I have to come
gelmelisin	you have to come
gelmeli	he has to come
gelmeliyiz	we have to come
gelmelisiniz	you have to come
gelmeliler	they have to come

The use of this form is rather like 'verb + **-ME** + possessive + **lazım**': **gelmeliyim/gelmem lazım**, but generally speaking **-MELİ** indicates a stronger degree of necessity than forms with **lazım**.

Yeni bir gömlek almam lazım. I need to buy a new shirt.
Yeni bir gömlek almalıyım. I must buy a new shirt.
(If the necessity is even stronger, then the word **şart** is used with 'verb
+ **-ME** + possessive': **Yeni bir gömlek almam şart.** 'I (absolutely)
have to buy a new shirt.')

Further examples with **-MELİ**:

Sizinle bu konuyu daha uzun konuşmalıyız.
We must discuss this matter further (with you).
İstanbul'a gidince Topkapı Sarayını görmelisiniz.
When you go to Istanbul you must see the Topkapı Palace.
Çok çalıştınız, onun için yorgun olmalısınız.
You have worked a lot, so you must be tired.

The negative form of **-MELİ** indicates a necessity *not to do* something:

Pencere açıkken kapıyı açmamalısınız.
You must not open the door while the window is open.
Güneşte fazla oturmamalısınız.
You must not sit in the sun a lot (a long time).
Note: This could also be **Güneşte fazla oturmamanız lazım**,
although it is more usual to use **-MELİ**, but if you wish to say 'it is not
necessary for you to sit in the sun', then **lazım değil** has to be used;
you cannot use **-MELİ**: **Güneşte oturmanız lazım değil.**

The third person singular form of **-MELİ** can be used impersonally to
mean 'one has to/one ought to/one should':

Anahtarı kapıda bırakmamalı. One should not leave the key in the
door.
Kütüphanede yüksek sesle konuşmamalı. One must not talk
loudly in the library.
Kırmızı ışıkta durmalı. One must stop at red lights.

Exercise 28

Translate:
1 I don't need this pillow; would you like it?
2 We have to leave early to be there at half past nine.

3 You have to learn Turkish in order to speak to (with) your Turkish
    friends.
4 You must not switch the radio on after twelve o'clock at night.
5 I must give him some money.

Vocabulary

dikkat etmek	to pay attention (to)
özellikle	especially
ışın	ray
kuvvet	strength
kuvvetli	strong
yakıcı	burning
dikkatli olmak	to be careful
uygun	suitable, convenient
deri	skin
hastalık	disease
bol	plenty, plentiful
vücut	body
su	water
tehlikeli	dangerous
geçirmek	to spend (time etc., *not* money); to see someone off
yanmak	to burn, get tanned
güneşlenmek	to sunbathe
koruyucu	protective
krem	cream
sürmek	to smear, spread (also: to drive; to last)
zevkli	pleasant
rahat	comfortable

READING

Yaz aylarında tatile giderken bazı şeylere dikkat etmek gerekir. Özellikle
uzun süre güneşte kalmamalıdır. Güneş ışınları öğle saatlerinde çok
kuvvetli ve yakıcıdır, onun için güneş banyosu yaparken dikkatli olmalıdır.
Güneş banyosu için en uygun saatler on ikiden önce ve üç buçuktan
sonradır. Güneşte fazla yanmamak için güneşlenirken koruyucu kremler
sürmelidir. Ayrıca sıcakta bol su içmelidir, çünkü vücut su kaybeder.
Öğle yemeklerinde çok yiyip içki içmek ve ondan sonra denize girmek
tehlikelidir. Bunlara uyunca zevkli, rahat bir tatil geçirirsiniz.

Lesson 13

117 Participles

In English, relative pronouns, words like 'who', 'whom', 'which' etc., are used to form a longer sentence from two short ones.

Thus: The man is talking. The man is my friend.
becomes: The man who is talking is my friend.

The main noun – the recurrent element – in these two sentences is 'the man'. When the two sentences are joined, the word 'who' is used as a link to refer to 'the man' through the action he is engaged in: in this case, talking.

Turkish does not have words like 'who', 'whom', or 'which' to join sentences like this. Instead, suffixes are added to the verb to form adjectives, called participles, and these are used to connect such sentences. There are two basic types of participle: subject participles and object participles.

The subject participle

This is used where the recurrent element ('the man' in the above sentence) is the subject of the first sentence and where, if a person rather than a thing is involved, English would use 'who'. The sentence above would be put into Turkish as:

Konuşan adam arkadaşımdır. lit. The talking man is my friend.

The subject participle is also used where the recurrent element is the object of the second sentence, provided it is the subject of the first.

Thus: The man is talking. I know the man.
becomes: I know the man who is talking.

'The man' is the object of the second sentence. But because it is the subject of the first, English still uses 'who', and Turkish again uses the subject participle.

Konuşan adamı tanıyorum.

Of course, if the recurrent element is a thing rather than a person, English will use the relative pronoun 'which'.

Thus: The bus goes to Ankara. The bus is delayed.
becomes: The bus which goes to Ankara is delayed.

Turkish will still use the subject participle if the recurrent element is the subject of the first sentence (the subject of the English relative clause):

Ankara'ya giden otobüs gecikti.

The subject participles are discussed in sections 118 to 123 below.

The object participle

The second type of participle, the object participle, is used to link other pairs of sentences, where the recurrent element (in the example that follows, 'the man') is not the subject of the first sentence (the sentence which in English becomes the relative clause when the two sentences are joined).

I saw the man last night. The man is Turkish.
The man (whom) I saw last night is Turkish.

Here the recurrent element, 'the man', is the object of the first sentence, although it is the subject of the second. English uses 'whom' rather than 'who' in this case, and Turkish uses the object participle:

Dün gece gördüğüm adam Türktür.

The object participle is also used where English would use other relative pronouns like 'where', 'when' etc. The object participles are discussed in the next lesson.

Formation of participles

Participles are always made by adding suffixes to verbs. If there is no full verb, the verb base **ol-** is used, and suffixes are added to form participles (see examples under different participles). Different participle suffixes are used to indicate the time of the action in relation to the time of the main verb.

118 -(Y)EN: present participle

This suffix forms the most frequently used subject participle. Its variants are **-yen**, **-yan** after vowels, and **-en**, **-an** after consonants. It generally indicates action taking place at the same time as the main verb, so although it is called the present participle it can express action in the past if the main verb is in the past.

İstasyonda bekleyen kadın Ankara'ya gidiyordu. The woman who was waiting at the station was going to Ankara. (lit. The at-the-station-waiting woman was going to Ankara.)
Türkiye'ye giden arkadaşlarımız her zaman bu otelde kalıyor. Our friends who go to Turkey always stay at this hotel. (lit. Our to-Turkey-going friends ...)
Masada duran mektupları postaya atacağım. I shall post the letters that are (standing) on the table.
Sizinle konuşan adam kimdi? Who was the man who was talking with (to) you?

A participle does not always have to be followed by a noun. In such cases a non-specific noun like 'person', 'people', 'thing' or 'one' is assumed to be there:

Telefon eden kimdi? Who was it who rang?
Yemeğe gelenler çiçek getirdi. Those who came to dinner brought flowers.
Burada Türkçe konuşan var mı? Is there anyone here who speaks Turkish?
En ucuz olan hangisi? Which is it that is the cheapest?

In negative constructions, participles follow the negative suffix:

Çok pahalı olmayan bir hediye almak istiyorum. I want to buy a present which is not very expensive.
Et yemeyenler için bir çok sebze yemekleri var. There are numerous vegetable dishes for those who do not eat meat.

119 -MİŞ: past participle

The participle formed by this suffix refers to actions that occurred before the action expressed by the main verb. It is identical with the reported past suffix, and its variants are **-miş**, **-mış**, **-müş** and **-muş**.

Çok iyi pişmiş bir tavuk yedik. We had (ate) a very well cooked chicken.

This participle is often coupled with **olan**, especially if the noun qualified by the participle is human.

Biletlerini almış olanlar kapıda beklemedi. Those who had bought their tickets did not wait at the door.

İstanbul'a daha önce gelmiş olan turistler değişik şeyler görmek istiyor. Tourists who have been to Istanbul previously want to see different things.

Mektubumu almamış olan otel bize bir oda ayırmamış. The hotel, which had not received my letter, had not reserved a room for us.

İki yıl önce yapılmış olan bu bina şehrin en büyük otelidir. This building which was built two years ago is the largest hotel in the town.

In the newspapers you may often see the past participle **-MIŞ** followed by **bulunan**, which is almost the same as **olan**:

Dün Ankara'ya gelmiş bulunan başbakan bugün parlamentoda bir konuşma yaptı. The Prime Minister, who came to Ankara yesterday, made a speech in parliament today.

In this sentence, instead of **gelmiş bulunan** we could use **gelmiş olan** or **gelen** (remember, the **-(Y)EN** participle is used for the past as well as present), and the meaning would still be the same.

Notice the nouns formed with this participle suffix:

dolmuş   a shared taxi
geçmiş   the past

120 -(Y)ECEK: future participle

This participle suffix, which is identical with the future tense, is used to refer to actions that will happen in the future in relation to the time expressed by the main verb, and also the time the sentence is uttered. Its variants are **-yecek** and **-yacak** after vowels, **-ecek** and **-acak** after consonants. Like the past participle **-MİŞ**, the future participle is frequently coupled with **olan**.

Londra'dan sabah sekizde kalkacak (olan) uçak üç buçuk saat

sonra Dalaman havaalanına inecek. The plane which will take off from London at eight in the morning will land at Dalaman airport three and a half hours later.
Bizimle çalışacak (olan) adam İngilizmiş. The man who is going to work with us is apparently British.

Sometimes when the noun to be qualified is not directly the doer of the action referred to by the verb carrying the participle, **olan** is not used:

Bu kitabı okuyacak vaktim yok. I do not have time to read this book.
Yiyecek ne var? What is there to eat?
Olanlardan sonra söyleyecek bir şey kalmadı. After all that happened, there is nothing left to say.

Some nouns formed with this participle suffix are:

gelecek the future
alacak money owed to one, credit
açacak any tool for opening a bottle or can (either of these can be specified in compounds):
    konserve açacağı can-opener
    şişe açacağı bottle opener

121 The aorist participle

The aorist (timeless) participle has the same variants as the aorist tense (section 84). It is used for conditions that are permanent or inherent qualities of the noun it qualifies. However, its function can equally be fulfilled by the present participle **-(Y)EN**:

Türkçe'ye benzer bir dil var mı? Is there a language like Turkish?
Türkçe'ye benzeyen bir dil var mı? Is there a language like Turkish?

Because of this overlapping of functions, the aorist participle suffix is not used with every verb – and where it is used, the words formed have, in many cases, come to be used as established nouns and adjectives.

gelir income
gider expenditure
yazar author
okur reader
okuryazar educated (**okuryazar bir kişi**: an educated person)
akarsu running water, watercourse

Its negative form can also be used in this way:

çıkmaz sokak   cul-de-sac
tükenmez kalem   ball-point pen
bitmez tükenmez   endless

Exercise 29

Translate:
1 The plane that goes to Dalaman is full.
2 The buses that stop here go to Ephesus (Efes).
3 Those who have stayed here want to come again.
4 He apparently has no time to see us tomorrow.
5 I want a bag similar to yours.

122 Subject participles from possessives

The subject participle is also used for 'whose' and 'of which' in constructions where there is a possessive, and the main noun which has the possessive suffix (the noun possessed) is the subject of the construction. Consider the following sentence:

Kızın babası bize kitap veriyor. The girl's father is giving us books.

Although **kızın babası** together constitutes the subject of the sentence, **babası** is the essential subject and has the possessive suffix (it is the noun possessed by **kızın**). So if we turn this sentence into a clause (to go into a longer sentence) we use a subject participle. In the example we have, this subject participle is **-(Y)EN** (present participle):

babası bize kitap veren kız the girl whose father gives us books (lit. her-father-to-us-book-giving girl)

In the examples below you have full sentences which are then turned into clauses:

Kadının kocası Türkiye'de çalışıyor. The woman's husband works in Turkey.
kocası Türkiye'de çalışan kadın the woman whose husband works in Turkey (lit. her-husband-in-Turkey-working woman)

Yaşlı adamın köpeği havlıyor. The old man's dog is barking.
köpeği havlayan yaşlı adam the old man whose dog is barking (lit.
his-dog-barking old man)
Adamın evi depremde çökmedi. The man's house did not collapse
in the earthquake.
evi depremde çökmeyen adam the man whose house did not
collapse in the earthquake

Subject participles other than **-(Y)EN** are also often used, with the
word **olan** after them:

Turistlerin uçağı sekizde kalkacak. The tourists' plane will take off
at eight.
uçağı sekizde kalkacak olan turistler the tourists whose plane will
take off at eight

When a clause is made from an original sentence which does not contain
a full verb, the participle suffixes are coupled to the verb base **ol-**:

Adamın evi çok büyük. The man's house is very big.
evi çok büyük olan adam the man whose house is very big
Otelin havuzu derin değil. The pool of the hotel is not deep.
havuzu derin olmayan otel the hotel the pool of which is not deep

fiyatları ucuz olan ceketler the jackets the prices of which are cheap
karısı Türk olmayan adam the man whose wife is not Turkish
hastası ölmeyecek olan doktor the doctor whose patient is not going
to die
içi boş olan kutu the box the inside of which is empty
dışı beyaz olan ev the house the outside of which is white

Exercise 30

Translate:
1 Our friend whose house is in Kaş wants to come to Britain.
2 The passengers whose suitcases are still at the hotel are getting on the
bus to go to the airport.
3 The room the windows of which are closed is very stuffy (without
air).
4 We stayed at a hotel the food (meals) of which was very delicious.
5 I don't like this jacket which has no pockets.

123 Derivational suffixes: -LEŞ and -LE

Both these suffixes derive verbs from non-verbs.

-LEŞ

This has the meaning of becoming or acquiring the quality of
something. Its variants are **-leş** and **-laş**.

güzel	beautiful	**güzelleşmek**	to become beautiful
iri	large, big	**irileşmek**	to become large, big
yabancı	a foreigner	**yabancılaşmak**	to become alienated
bir	one	**birleşmek**	to become one, unite

Kitaplarımı içine koyunca çantam ağırlaştı. When I put my
books in it, my bag became heavier.
Yirmi dakikadan fazla kaynayan çorba koyulaştı. The soup
which boiled for over twenty minutes thickened.
Koyulaşan çorbaya üç bardak su ilave ettik. We added three
glasses of water to the soup which had thickened.

-LE

A large number of verbs are formed with this suffix. Its variants are **-le**
and **-la**. In general it means to do or to make what the word to which it
is attached stands for.

temiz	clean	**temizlemek**	to clean
hazır	ready	**hazırlamak**	to prepare
kuru	dry	**kurulamak**	to dry
su	water	**sulamak**	to water
bağ	tie	**bağlamak**	to tie
parça	piece	**parçalamak**	to break into pieces
geri	backward	**gerilemek**	to retreat, go backwards

Sorumu yineledim ama cevap vermedi. I repeated my question but
he did not answer.
**Kar başlayınca yolumuza devam etmedik ve yakındaki bir
köyde geceledik.** When the snow started, we did not continue with
our journey and spent the night in a nearby village.

144

CONVERSATION

– Affedersiniz, Ankara'ya giden otobüs nereden kalkıyor?
– Ankara'ya bir saat içinde iki otobüs var, biri Bursa üzerinden, biri Bolu üzerinden. Sizinki hangisi?
– Benimki Bolu üzerinden olan.
– Bolu üzerinden gidecek otobüs şu binanın yanından kalkıyor. Biraz sonra gelir.
– Teşekkür ederim.

üzerinden   via, over

Exercise 31

Translate:

1 After drying the cups, I put them in the cupboard beside the window.
2 Have you packed (lit. prepared) your suitcase?
3 Despite your having lived (resided) outside Turkey for twenty years, you have not become alienated.
4 Those who were suntanned (got burnt in the sun) became more beautiful.
5 He asked me to repeat my question.

Lesson 14

124 Object participles

In lesson 13, we said that object participles are used where two sentences to be linked have different subjects, as in the English sentences:

The police (subject) caught the man.
The man (subject) was not a thief.
The man whom the police caught was not a thief.

In this combined sentence, the recurrent element (the noun which occurred in both of the simple sentences that were joined) 'the man' is the subject of the main verb (was) and the object of the verb in the relative clause (caught).

In such cases an object participle is used in Turkish to join the two sentences, because the recurrent element is the object of the sentence that becomes the clause. In fact, the object participles are also used in Turkish when the recurrent element is not the direct object of the subordinate clause, and when English uses another relative pronoun like 'where' or 'to whom':

The house where they live is too small.
The man I gave the book to has gone. (The man to whom I gave the book has gone.)

There are two participles which function in this manner in Turkish, and they are both followed by the possessive suffix. The possessive suffix in this case indicates the doer of the action, that is to say the subject of the participle. The literal meaning of the Turkish versions of the two sentences above will thus be:

The their-living-house is too small.
The the-book-my-having-given man has gone.

125 -DİK + possessive: past/present object participle

This participle suffix covers a wide variety of time references: it is used in place of the past, aorist and continuous (**-(İ)YOR**) tenses. The context and the tense of the main verb have to be considered when translating it into English.

As the suffix is always immediately followed by a possessive suffix, the **k** in **-DİK** changes to **ğ**, except when followed by the third person plural possessive **-LERİ**. Variants of **-DİK** are **-tik, -tık, -tük** and **-tuk** after verbs ending in voiceless consonants, and **-dik, dık, -dük** and **duk** elsewhere.

Thus the two examples we gave above are translated as follows:

The house where they live is too small. **Oturdukları ev fazla küçüktür.**
The man I gave the book to has gone. **Kitabı verdiğim adam gitti.**

Here are some further examples, with literal translations of the Turkish:

İttiğim kapı adama çarptı. The door which I pushed hit the man. (lit. The my-having-pushed door hit the man.)
Bahçeye astığın havlular yağmurda ıslandı. The towels which you hung in the garden got wet in the rain. (lit. The in-the-garden your-having-hung towels got wet in the rain.)
Elinden tuttuğu çocuk birdenbire caddeye fırladı. The child whom she was holding by the hand suddenly rushed into the road. (lit. The by-its-hand her-having-held child suddenly rushed into the road.)
Beklediğimiz haber bugün gelmeyecek. The news we expect will not come today. (lit. The our-having-expected news will not come today.)
Masaya koyduğunuz mektuplar kimin? Whose are the letters which you put on the table? (lit. The on-the-table your-having-put letters are whose?)

Because this type of participle is always followed by the possessive suffix, a genitive suffix earlier in the sentence is always implied (as we found when considering the possessive suffix, section 43). In the above sentences, the genitive would be the genitive pronoun of the same person as the participle with its possessive ending:

(Benim) ittiğim kapı adama çarptı.

(Senin) bahçeye astığın havlular yağmurda ıslandı.
(Onun) elinden tuttuğu çocuk ...
(Bizim) beklediğimiz haber ...

In these sentences, the meaning of the pronoun is understood in the suffix, and the pronoun (**benim, senin, onun, bizim** etc.) can be omitted. But if the possessive is in the third person singular or plural, and it refers to a word other than **onun** or **onların** (which can be omitted), then that word must be included and must be in the genitive. Thus the sentence above:

Masaya koyduğunuz mektuplar kimin?

has the genitive at the end: **kimin?**

Ayşe'nin elinden tuttuğu çocuk caddeye fırladı. The child whom Ayşe was holding by the hand rushed into the road (lit. The by-its-hand Ayşe's-having-held child...)
Köpeğin ısırdığı çocuk ağlıyor. The child whom the dog bit is crying.
Trenlerin durduğu her istasyonda otopark var. At every station where the trains stop, there is a car park.

The genitive pronouns can actually be included in the sentence if a special emphasis or a contrast is intended:

Benim okuduğum kitap uzun, senin okuduğun kitap kısa. The book that I am reading is long, the book that you are reading is short.
Onun söylediği şey başka, senin söylediğin şey başka. The thing that he says is different, the thing that you say is different. (i.e. He says one thing, you are saying something else.)

Here are some examples to show how a sentence can be turned into the Turkish equivalent of a relative clause by means of **-DİK** + possessive suffix:

Ali dün yeni bir işe başladı.
Yesterday Ali started a new job.

Ali'nin dün başladığı yeni iş
the new job which Ali started yesterday

Kalabalık bir otobüse bindim.
I got on a crowded bus.

bindiğim kalabalık otobüs
the crowded bus that I got on

Orhan çantasını arkadaşına verdi.
Orhan gave his bag to his friend.

Orhan'ın çantasını verdiği arkadaşı
his friend to whom Orhan gave his bag

148

Ben bu katın sahibiyim.
I am the owner of this flat.

sahibi olduğum bu kat
this flat of which I am the owner

(Notice the verb **olmak** with the participle suffix in the last example: **sahibiyim** is made up of noun + personal suffix. The participle suffix can only be added to verbs, so the verb **olmak** is used for the clause as a peg on which to hang the participle suffix.)

Here are some examples with the verb in the negative:

Adamı tanımıyordum.
I did not know the man.
Elmayı yemediniz.
You did not eat the apple.
Mektupları saat ondan önce açmıyoruz.
We do not open the letters before 10 o'clock.

tanımadığım adam
the man whom I did not know
yemediğiniz elma
the apple that you did not eat
saat ondan önce açmadığımız mektuplar
the letters that we do not open before ten o'clock

126 -(Y)ECEK + possessive: future participle

The suffix **-(Y)ECEK** is used for the future tense and as a subject participle with future reference. As an object participle its reference is again future.

Bu akşam telefon edeceğim arkadaşım Türk. My friend whom I shall ring this evening is Turkish.
Çocukların gideceği okul uzak değil. The school that the children will go to is not far.
Size söyleyeceğim şeyi ona söylemeyin. Do not tell him the thing that I am going to tell you.

Further examples:

Doktordan randevu alacağım.
I shall get an appointment from the doctor.
10 numaralı otobüse bineceğim.
I shall get on the number 10 bus.

doktordan alacağım randevu
the appointment that I shall get from the doctor
bineceğim 10 numaralı otobüs
the number 10 bus that I shall get on

Some sentences in the negative:

Senin için yapmayacağım şey yok. There is nothing I won't do for you.
Ona beğenmeyeceği bir hediye vermek istemiyorum. I do not want to give him a present that he will not like.
Toplantıda konuşmayacağım kimse olmayacak. There will not be anyone at the meeting whom I shall not speak to.

Like the subject participles (see section 118) object participles can also occur without a noun following them; it is understood that a 'person', 'thing' or 'one' is implied here:

Pazar günleri en çok sevdiğim geç kalkmaktır. The thing that I like most on Sundays is to get up late.
Onun bilmediği yok. There is nothing (not a thing) that he does not know.

127 Object participles from possessives

Object participles are also used to mean 'of whom', 'of which' in possessive constructions where the main noun which has the possessive suffix is *not* the subject of the construction:

Arkadaşımın evinde kaldım. I stayed at my friend's house.

In this sentence **evinde** has the possessive suffix, but it is not the subject of the sentence (the subject is 'I', which is indicated by the personal suffix of the verb). Therefore when this sentence is turned into a clause, an object participle has to be added to the verb, giving us:

evinde kaldığım arkadaşım my friend in whose house I stayed (lit. in the house of him my-having-stayed my friend)
Bu lokantanın yemeğini çok seviyorum. I very much like the food in (lit. of) this restaurant.
yemeğini çok sevdiğim lokanta the restaurant the food of which I very much like
Halının yerini değiştireceğim. I shall change the position of the carpet.
yerini değiştireceğim halı the carpet the position of which I shall change

Here are some further examples:

üstünü topladığım masa the table the top of which I tidied up
ortasında toplandığımız meydan the square in the middle of which
we gathered
bakışlarından korktuğum adam the man of whose looks I was
frightened (lit. the from-his-looks I-was-frightened man)

Exercise 32

Translate:
1 The man I saw in front of the house was a thief.
2 The meal we ate at the restaurant was not expensive.
3 I have also read the book you are reading now.
4 Do you know the name of the hotel where you'll stay?
5 The film that we are going to see is about (shows) the British who
work in Turkey.

128 'when' with object participles

'When' is expressed by:

-DİK } + possessive + { **zaman**
-(Y)ECEK } { **vakit**

Televizyonu açtığım zaman program bitmişti. When I turned
the TV on, the programme had ended. (lit. At the time of my having
turned on the TV, the programme had ended.)
Paramız olduğu zaman dışarda yemek yiyoruz. When we have
money, we eat out.
Onlar geldikleri zaman çok geç olacak. It will be very late (or: too
late) when they come.
Hesabı ödeyeceğiniz zaman garsonu çağırın. Call the waiter
when you are going to pay the bill.
Hazır olduğunuz zaman gideriz. We go when you are ready.

Although the word **vakit** is interchangeable with **zaman**, in general
zaman is used more frequently, especially in writing.

The words **sıra** or **sırada**, 'time', 'at the time', are also used similarly; the implication is that there is a greater immediacy to the action, which can often be translated as 'just as':

Kapıdan çıktığım sırada yağmur başladı. The rain started just as I went out of the door.
Yağmur başladığı sırada biz denizdeydik. We were in the sea just as the rain started.
Yemek yiyeceğimiz sırada misafir geldi. Just as we were about to eat, we had visitors (guests arrived).

Notice that in this kind of construction the genitive is not used:

Şoförler grev yaptığı zaman otobüsler çalışmaz. When the drivers go on strike, the buses do not run.
Film başladığı sırada elektrikler söndü. The lights went out just as the film started.

Şoförler and **film** do not take the genitive ending.

129 Object participles as nouns

In the forms we have seen so far, the object participles, together with the relevant possessive suffixes added to them, function like adjectives qualifying the noun that follows. And even when a noun is not actually present we know that there is an implied noun form (like 'person' or 'thing') which the object participle qualifies. However, the same suffixes can also make the verb to which they are added function like a noun, so that in fact the whole clause has the function of a noun. The suffixes which any ordinary noun may take follow the object participle + noun combination as necessary. Often the Turkish can be translated literally into a rather old-fashioned, stilted English.

Senin geldiğini duymadım. I did not hear you come (lit. your coming).
Türkçe konuştuğumu kimse bilmiyor. No one knows that I speak Turkish. (lit. No one knows my speaking Turkish.)
Çantanızı kaybettiğinize üzüldüm. I am sorry that you lost your bag. (lit. I am sorry at your having lost your bag.)
Para vermeyeceklerinden korkuyordum. I was afraid that they would not pay. (lit. I was afraid of their not being about to pay.)

152

Yazın Akdeniz bölgesinin çok sıcak olduğunu biliyorum. I know
that the Mediterranean region is very hot in the summer. (lit. I am
aware of the Mediterranean region's being very hot in summer.)

The above structures are rather like verbal nouns formed with the **-ME**
suffix (section 113) insofar as in both cases the verb functions like a noun.
However, while the structures formed with these participle suffixes
represent a fact, an action which has taken place or will definitely take
place, those formed with the verbal noun suffix **-ME** indicate an action as
an idea, not an actual happening, or as the concept or way of doing
something.

Kadının yemek yediğini görmedim. I did not see the woman eat
(that the woman ate).
Kadının yemek yemesini görmedim. I did not see the way the
woman eats.
Öğretmen Ayşe'nin çok çalıştığını söyledi. The teacher said that
Ayşe worked very hard.
Öğretmen Ayşe'nin çok çalışmasını söyledi. The teacher told
Ayşe to work very hard.
John'un Türkçe konuştuğunu duymadım. I did not hear John
speak Turkish. (I did not hear him actually speaking Turkish.)
John'un Türkçe konuşmasını duymadım. I did not hear the way
John speaks Turkish.

130 Indirect speech

Object participles are used in indirect (or reported) speech, when
something said or written by someone is quoted indirectly.

Direct: **Başbakan, "Türkiye Avrupa Topluluğu'na girecektir"
dedi.** The Prime Minister said: "Turkey will enter the
European Community".

Indirect: **Başbakan Türkiye'nin Avrupa Topluluğu'na
gireceğini söyledi.** The Prime Minister said that Turkey
would enter the E.C.

Direct: **Lokantadaki garson "Balık çok taze" dedi.** The waiter
in the restaurant said: "The fish is very fresh".

Indirect: **Lokantadaki garson balığın çok taze olduğunu söyledi.**
The waiter in the restaurant said that the fish was very fresh.

When an imperative sentence is put into indirect (reported) speech, however, the verbal noun form with **-ME** is used:

Direct: **Satıcı "Parayı kasaya ödeyin" dedi.** The sales-person said: "Pay at the cash desk".

Indirect: **Satıcı parayı kasaya ödememi söyledi.** The sales-person told me to pay at the cash desk.

If the last example above were formed with the participle suffixes **-DİK** or **-(Y)ECEK** the meaning of the sentence would be quite different:

Satıcı parayı kasaya ödediğimi söyledi. The sales-person said that I had paid (the money) at the cash desk.
Satıcı parayı kasaya ödeyeceğimi söyledi. The sales-person said that I would pay (the money) at the cash desk.

In both cases the paying of the money is action that has happened or is due to happen definitely, and is therefore a fact, not a notion.

131 whether ... or not

This construction is formed by using the same verb twice, first with the **-(Y)İP** suffix (section 108) and then immediately afterwards with the **-ME** negative suffix followed by the appropriate verbal noun or participle and personal suffix; a case suffix may also follow if needed.

Bu dili öğrenip öğrenmemeniz önemli değil. It is not important whether you learn this language or not.
Çamaşır makinasının çalışıp çalışmadığını bilmiyorum. I do not know whether the washing machine works or not.
Yarın gelip gelmeyeceklerini söylemediler. They did not say whether they will come tomorrow or not.
Soruları anlayıp anlamayacağınıza göre yeniden tekrarlayacağım. I shall repeat the questions depending on whether you (will) understand them or not.

Vocabulary

ısmarlamak	to order (in restaurant/café), to treat someone to something
konser	concert
taşımak	to carry

doldurmak	to fill, fill in
gümrük memuru	customs officer
memur	official, clerk
unutmak	to forget
bakır	copper
tepsi	tray
geç kalmak	to be late
Türk Havayolları (THY)	Turkish Airlines
İngiliz Havayolları	British Airways

Exercise 33

Translate:

1 Kahve ısmarladığım adamın adını bilmiyorum, ama sen onu çok iyi tanıyorsun.
2 Üstünü kapadığım tencerede yemek yoktu.
3 Gitmek istediğimiz konsere bilet kalmamış.
4 Bavulunu taşıdığın kadın nereye gidiyor?
5 Dolduracağınız kâğıdı gümrük memuruna vereceksiniz.
6 The woman whose name I forgot gave me this copper tray.
7 He said I was twenty minutes late.
8 The customs officer asked me to open my suitcase.
9 He didn't know I was here.
10 They said they would be coming by Turkish Airlines; British Airways planes were apparently full.

132 Combinations with -DİK/-(Y)ECEK + possessive

With 'için': because (of), as

Param olmadığı için sana bir hediye almadım. Because I did not have any money, I did not buy you a present.

Yarın misafir geleceği için yemek yapmam lazım. As guests will come tomorrow, I have to cook (lit. make food)

Pikniğe sizin de geleceğinizi bilmediğim için fazla sandviç getirmedim. As I did not know that you too were coming to the picnic, I did not bring a lot of sandwiches.

Kedi, balığı yediği için bize kalmadı. Because the cat ate the fish, there was none left for us.

155

With 'halde': although

Hava soğuk olduğu halde üşümüyorum. Although the weather is cold, I am not cold.

Çorba sevmediğiniz halde niçin ısmarladınız? Although you do not like soup, why did you order (it)?

Bunu sana yine anlatacağım halde anlamayacaksın, çünkü ben de çok iyi bilmiyorum. Although I shall explain this to you again, you will not understand it, because I do not know it very well either.

With 'kadar': as much as, as ... as

Bu iş senin sandığın kadar kolay değil. This task is not as easy as you think.

İstediğiniz kadar için. Drink as much as you like.

Durum söyledikleri kadar kötü değil. The situation is not as bad as they said.

With 'gibi': like, as

İstediğiniz gibi hareket edin, ben karışmıyorum. You act/behave as you like, I am not interfering.

Az sonra göreceğiniz gibi bu harabeler çok iyi durumdadır. As you will see a little later, these ruins are in very good condition.

With '-(Y)E göre': according to, as

Haberlerden anladığıma göre gelecek hafta havaalanlarında grev var. According to what I understood from the news, there is a strike at the airports next week.

Bu sorunun cevabını bildiğine göre niçin söylemiyorsun? As you know the answer to this question, why do you not say (i.e. give the answer)?

Ali'nin mektubunda yazdığına göre Kaş'ta havalar çok güzelmiş. According to what Ali writes in his letter, the weather is very good in Kaş.

With '-DEN başka': other than, apart from

Size verdiğimden başka iki şişe daha var. Apart from what (the one that) I gave you, there are two bottles more.
Söylediğinizden başka bir şey var mı? Is there anything else apart from what you said (told)?

With 'takdirde': in the event of

Erken geldiğiniz takdirde beni girişte bekleyin lütfen. In the event of your coming early, please wait for me at the entrance.
Para verdikleri takdirde burada kalabilirler. In the event of their paying, they can stay here.

This is a rather formal expression and therefore used sparingly. It can also be translated as 'if'.

Vocabulary

ödemek	to pay	**doğum günü**	birthday
elektrikli eşya	electrical goods	**ummak**	} to hope
anahtar	key	**ümit etmek**	
paket	parcel, packaging	**ümit**	} hope
yeter	enough, sufficient	**umut**	
beden	size	**taşınmak**	to move
numara	number, figure		(house)
	(here: size)	**enflasyon**	inflation
bebek	baby, doll	**yüksek**	high
	(here: doll)		

CONVERSATION

Gümrükte

- Pasaportunuz lütfen.
- Buyurun.
- Türkiye'de ne kadar kalacaksınız?
- Üç hafta kadar.
- Hangi bavullar sizin?
- Bu siyah bavul.
- Gümrük ödemeniz gereken bir şey var mı?
- Sanmıyorum.
- Elektrikli eşya var mı?

- Yok.
- Bavulunuzu açar mısınız lütfen?
- Peki, bir dakika lütfen, anahtarı bulayım... Buyurun, bakın.
- Ne çok gömlek böyle... Üç hafta için biraz fazla değil mi? Hem bunlar daha paketlerinde.
- Üç hafta kalacağım için ancak yeter. Hem de üç dört tanesini evinde kalacağım arkadaşıma vereceğim.
- Bunlar hepsi aynı beden.
- Arkadaşıma sordum; mektupta yazdığına göre aynı numarayı giyiyormuşuz. Bu bebeği de arkadaşımın kızına aldım. Gelecek hafta doğum günü var, altı yaşında olacak.
- Bu söylediklerinizden başka hediye var mı?
- Hayır, hepsi bu.
- Peki, buyurun geçin. İyi tatiller.
- Teşekkür ederim.

Exercise 34

Translate:

1 The hotel where we stayed was not as comfortable as we had hoped.
2 As you know, we moved to this house last year.
3 According to what my friend says, inflation is high in Turkey.
4 Apart from the one I bought, there were two more jackets in the store.
5 In the event of your not coming, I will give the tickets to him.

Lesson 15

133 -(Y)EBİL: can, to be able to, may

This suffix is added to verbs to indicate that a certain action can be done, or that it is possible to perform that action. It is a combination of two forms: -(Y)E and -BİL, which comes from the verb **bilmek** 'to know'. This part of the ending is always -bil, it does not harmonise with the base. The variants of -(Y)EBİL are -yebil, -yabil after vowels, and -ebil, -abil after consonants. It is always followed by a tense suffix, often the aorist.

Mektup yazabilirim.   I am able to write a letter.
I can write a letter.
I may write a letter.

Saat sekizde gelebilir misiniz? Can you come at eight o'clock?
Caminin içinde fotoğraf çekebilir miyim? May I (Is it possible for me to) take pictures inside the mosque?
Üç ay sonra Türkçe konuşabileceksiniz. You will be able to speak Turkish after three months.
Uçak çok gecikti ama akşam yemeğinden önce otelimize varabildik. The plane was very late, but we were able to arrive at our hotel before dinner.
Dikkat et, sıcak olabilir, sonra elin yanar. Be careful, it may be hot, then your hand would burn.
Pencereyi açabilir miyim? May I open the window?

The negative of -(Y)EBİL is formed in two ways with different meanings, as described in the following sections.

134 -(Y)EME: cannot, unable to

This is formed with -(Y)E plus the negative suffix -ME and indicates that a certain action *cannot* be done, or that the subject of the verb is not able to do the action stated by the verb. It always follows the verb and it precedes the tense endings. Its variants are -yeme or -yama after vowels, and -eme or -ama after consonants.

Sabahları erken kalkamam. I cannot get up early in the mornings.
Bu akşam gelemem, ama yarın akşam gelirim. I cannot come this evening, but I can come tomorrow evening.

Before the tense suffix **-(İ)YOR**, the **-me** in **-(Y)EME** is spelt as **-mi** or **-mı** (see section 59):

Bir yıldır İstanbul'da oturuyor ama Türkçe konuşamıyor. He has been living in Istanbul for a year, but he cannot speak Turkish.
Hasta olduğu için denize giremiyor. He cannot go in the sea as he is ill.

Further examples:

Doktor çok meşgul, onun için sizi hemen göremeyecek. The doctor is very busy, so he will not be able to see you at once.
Söylediklerimi anlayamadılar. They could not understand what I said.
Adres doğruymuş ama evi bulamamış. The address was apparently correct, but he could not find the house (so I understand).
Olamaz. It cannot be. It is not possible. (indicates disbelief)
Benimle böyle konuşamazsınız. You cannot speak to me like this.
Film bugün başlıyor, daha önce görmüş olamaz. The film starts (is released) today, it is not possible that he has seen it before.
Çok vitamin alıyor, artık hasta olamaz. He is taking a lot of vitamins, he cannot (will not) be ill any more.

The suffixes **-(Y)EME** and **-(Y)EBİL** are put together to mean 'may not be able to'. This combined form is mostly used with the aorist tense suffix.

Çok işim var, hepsini yarına kadar bitiremeyebilirim. I have a lot of work, I may not be able to finish all of it by tomorrow.
Lokantada yer ayırtmak iyi olur, boş masa bulamayabiliriz. It would be (a) good (idea) to make a reservation at the restaurant, we may not be able to find a free table.
Jeton almadığı için telefon edemeyebilir. He may not be able to telephone as he did not buy telephone tokens.

160

135 -MEYEBİL: may not

This is the other form of the negative for **-(Y)EBİL** and indicates the possibility that an action *may not* be done. It comes after verbs and before tense suffixes. It is mostly used with the aorist. Its variants are **-meyebil** and **-mayabil**.

Beni beklemeyin, gelmeyebilirim. Do not wait for me, I may not come.

Parayı hemen almak lazım, sonra vermeyebilirler. It is necessary to take (one must take) the money at once, they may not give (it) later on.

Bugün Pazar, evde olmayabilirler. Today is Sunday, they may not be at home.

A past tense suffix can be added to the present to mean 'might':

Zili çok çaldığınız iyi oldu, duymayabilirdim. It was a good thing that you rang the bell a lot, I might not have heard it.

The following sentences illustrate the different uses of the suffixes given in this lesson:

Gelebilirim.	I can/may/am able to come.
Gelemem.	I cannot come./I am unable to come.
Gelemeyebilirim.	I may not be able to come.
Gelmeyebilirim.	It is possible that I may not come.

Exercise 35

1 Don't come to the airport, the plane may be delayed. We'll take (lit. get on) a taxi.
2 Can you wait ten minutes?
3 May I ask you something?
4 I looked at the newspaper, but I couldn't see that news.
5 Don't ring before six o'clock; he may not be at home.

136 Countries, languages, people

The names of most languages and nationalities are formed by adding two different suffixes to the names of the countries, or to adjectives relating to countries.

The suffix -Lİ

We saw earlier that the suffix -Lİ added to a place name indicates a person from that area (section 28). When added to the name of a country, the suffix -Lİ indicates nationality, and it is only used for people.

Amerika	America	**Amerikalı**	American
Pakistan	Pakistan	**Pakistanlı**	Pakistani
Hollanda	Holland	**Hollandalı**	Dutch
Polonya	Poland	**Polonyalı**	Polish

In the above examples the English words describing nationality are also used to refer to goods, food etc. from these countries; for example 'American cars, Dutch tulips, Polish beer, Indian food'. In Turkish we either have different forms for these words, or we use the name of the country.

Amerikan arabası	American cars
Hollanda lalesi	Dutch tulips
Polonya birası	Polish beer
Hint yemeği	Indian food

The suffix -CE

This suffix indicates the language spoken in a country or by a group of people. Its variants are **-çe** or **-ça** after voiceless consonants and **-ce** or **-ca** elsewhere.

İspanyol	Spanish	**İspanyolca**	Spanish (language only)
İngiliz	English	**İngilizce**	English
Türk	Turkish	**Türkçe**	Turkish
Alman	German	**Almanca**	German
Fransız	French	**Fransızca**	French
Norveç	Norwegian/Norway	**Norveçce**	Norwegian
ne?	what?	**nece?**	what language?

137 Uses of -CE

Apart from indicating a language, the suffix **-CE** has other functions as well, and in all these uses it is unstressed.

1 It can be added to nouns to mean 'like' what that noun represents:

çocuk child   çocukça childish, like a child
Kırk yaşında adam ama çocukça davranıyor. He is a forty-year-old man, but he is behaving like a child.
dost friend   dostça friendly, like a friend
Aramızda çok dostça bir konuşma geçti. We had a very friendly talk.

2 It can be added to adjectives to intensify the meaning of the adjective or to form adverbs:

açık open   açıkça clearly
Her şeyi açıkça anladım. I understood everything clearly.
yavaş slow/quiet   yavaşça slowly/quietly
Kapıyı yavaşça açıp içeri girdi. He opened the door slowly/quietly and went inside.

In this combination the suffix -CE can also mean 'not quite but almost', '-ish', forming adjectives:

Zengince bir ailenin oğluydu. He was the son of a family that was fairly rich.

These two sentences show the different meanings of this suffix:

Bardakları temizce yıkadım. I washed the glasses really clean.
Temizce bir bardak bulup su içtim. I found a cleanish glass and drank some water.

The frequently used word oldukça 'quite, almost' is made with this suffix:

Bugün hava oldukça serin, yemeği içeride yiyelim. Today the weather is quite cool, let us eat the meal indoors (inside).

3 With pronouns -CE means 'in the opinion of', 'according to':

bence in my view
Bence bütün bu söyledikleriniz yanlış. In my view, all these things that you have said are wrong.
Sizce kim haklı? In your opinion, who is right?

Vocabulary

ayakkabı	shoe	**o takdirde**	in that case
çıkarmak	to take off	**geri vermek**	to give back,
ibadet	worship		return
ibadet yeri	place of worship	**ses**	voice
dolaşmak	to wander around	**yüksek sesle**	loudly
örtmek	to cover	**bağış**	donation
eşarp	scarf	**atmak**	to throw

READING

Türkiye'de bir camiye gittiğiniz zaman içeri girmeden önce ayakkabılarınızı çıkarmanız gerekir. Camiler ibadet yeri olduğu için içeride istediğiniz gibi dolaşamazsınız. Kadınların başlarını örtmeleri lazımdır. Yanınızda bir eşarp ya da başınızı örtecek bir şey olmayabilir. O takdirde oradaki bir görevliden bir başörtüsü isteyebilirsiniz, ve camiden çıkarken bunu geri verirsiniz. Camide yüksek sesle konuşmamalıdır. Fotoğraf çekmek için izin almak gerekebilir. Camilere giriş parasızdır. Bazı camilerde bir bağış kutusu vardır, isteyenler oraya para atabilir.

Exercise 36

Translate:

1 I learnt French at school, but I cannot speak (it) well.
2 In your opinion, is this correct?
3 Our Dutch friends want to learn Turkish.
4 As you want to learn English, you must come to Britain.
5 They couldn't sit down as they couldn't find a seat.

Lesson 16

138 The conditional: -SE

This suffix is added to verb bases; the only suffix that can precede it is the negative -ME. It operates like a tense suffix and takes the same personal endings as the past tense suffix -Dİ. It indicates unreal conditions: situations where the likelihood of something happening is remote, where you wish the action indicated by the verb taking the conditional -SE would happen, but you know that it is very unlikely.

gelsem	if I were to come	**okusam**	if I were to read
gelsen	if you were to come	**okusan**	if you were to read
gelse	if he were to come	**okusa**	if he were to read
gelsek	if we were to come	**okusak**	if we were to read
gelseniz	if you were to come	**okusanız**	if you were to read
gelseler	if they were to come	**okusalar**	if they were to read

Gelsen görürsün. If you were to come, you would see (it). (implying 'but you won't come')
Çok param olsa dünya turuna çıkarım. If I had a lot of money, I would go on a round-the-world tour (but I haven't).
Okusam anlardım. If I were to read it, I would understand it (but I haven't read it).
Türkçe bilmese gazeteyi okuyamaz. If he did not know Turkish, he could not read the newspaper (but he does).
Ali'ye ne olduğunu bilsek size söylerdik. If we knew what happened to Ali, we would have told you (but we don't).

It is also used in questions when we are wondering about something:

Ne giysem? What should I wear?
Saat kaçta telefon etsem? At what time should I ring?
Nerede buluşsak? Where should we meet?

In this sense, it is frequently accompanied by **acaba:**

Acaba ne söylesem? I wonder what I should say?
Ne yesek acaba? I wonder what we should eat?

It is also used with **de** and **bile** 'even':

Özür dilemek için telefon etse de onunla konuşmayacağım.
Even if he rings to apologise, I shall not speak to him.
Hemen çıksak bile trene yetişemeyiz.
Even if we were to leave at once, we could not catch the train.

The conditional phrases are sometimes preceded by the word **keşke**, which expresses regret:

Keşke bu kadar çok çalışmasa! If only he would not work so hard!
Onu çok özledim, keşke bir gün görsem! I missed her a lot, if only I might see her one day!

The suffix **-(Y)Dİ** can be added to **-SE** forming a past conditional, 'if only ... had':

Sinemaya giderken keşke bana da haber verseydiniz! I wish you had let me know when you went to the cinema (but you didn't).
Keşke başka bir yemek seçseydik! If only we had chosen another dish!

139 İSE/-(Y)SE: conditional of 'to be'

İSE functions like **İDİ** and takes the same set of personal suffixes. It indicates a real condition: a situation where the condition is quite likely true. It can stand by itself, but often it is suffixed as **-se** or **-sa** after bases ending in a consonant, and as **-yse** or **-ysa** after bases that end in a vowel.

Hastaysan okula gelme. If you are ill, do not come to school.
Evde değilse haber bırak. If he is not at home, leave a message.
Yorgun değilsek sinemaya gideriz, yorgunsak evde otururuz. If we are not tired we'll go to the cinema, if we are tired we'll stay at home.
Paran varsa bana biraz borç verir misin? If you have any money, can you lend me some?
İşiniz yoksa biraz konuşalım. If you have nothing (no work) to do, let's chat a little.

The interrogatives **nerede, ne** and **nasıl** have acquired different meanings with **-(Y)SE** added to them:

neredeyse almost (lit. wherever it is)
Saat neredeyse dokuz oldu. It is almost nine o'clock.
neyse anyway; anyhow; well, never mind (lit. whatever it is)
nasılsa somehow (lit. however it is)

-(Y)SE can follow any of the tense suffixes, but its most frequent use is with the aorist tense.

Biraz daha istersem alırım. If I want some more, I'll take (it).
Gelirseniz seviniriz. We'll be pleased if you come.
Toplantıya gelmeyecekseniz lütfen bana haber verir misiniz?
If you are not coming to the meeting, would you please let me know?
Uçakta yer bulabilirsek bu hafta sonu gitmek istiyoruz. If we can find seats on the plane, we want to leave this weekend.
Bu otelde kalmayacaklarsa nerede kalacaklar? If they will not stay at this hotel, where will they stay?

Note that the third person plural suffix **-LER** is put before the conditional and after the tense suffix: **kalmayacaklarsa.**

Yemeğini bitirmişse neden hesabı istemiyor? If he has finished his food, why does he not ask for the bill?
Çantanı masada bıraktıysan garsonlar bulmuştur. If you left your bag on the table, the waiters must have found it. (a certainty expressed by the use of the **-tur (-DİR)** suffix)

The word **eğer** 'if' is frequently used with conditional sentences; it is usually put at the beginning of the sentence and immediately alerts the listener that a conditional situation is to follow. It stresses the conditional situation: otherwise its use is optional.

Eğer anlayabiliyorsan mesele yok. If you are able to understand, there is no problem.
Eğer lokantada sizden çok para aldılarsa şikayet edebilirsiniz.
If they have charged you a lot in the restaurant, you can make a complaint.

Exercise 37

Translate into Turkish:
1 If he were to ring, I would tell him to come.
2 If I were to receive your letter, I would answer it.

3 If you are tired, don't come to the cinema.
4 If you (pl.) are not going to stay here, where will you stay?
5 If I work very hard I shall be rich.

140 Some derivational suffixes

-SEL

This suffix is added to nouns to form adjectives. It has been used to replace the suffix -İ which had been borrowed from Arabic and is still used with some words like:

asker	soldier	**askeri**	military
din	religion	**dini**	religious

The suffix **-SEL** is also used with the word **din**, forming the word **dinsel** 'religious'. Which to use has become a matter of personal choice. However, **-SEL** is not used with the word **asker**. Apart from such special cases **-SEL** is used very widely. Its variants are **-sel** and **-sal**.

kişi	person	**kişisel**	personal
birey	individual	**bireysel**	individual(istic)
tarih	history	**tarihsel**	historical
düş	dream	**düşsel**	imaginary, dreamy
para	money	**parasal**	monetary

-(İ)MTRAK

This suffix is mostly added to words indicating colour or taste, and means that a certain object is 'almost of that colour or taste'. The first vowel is not used if the base ends in a vowel, and the second part of the suffix does not change: it is non-harmonic.

sarı	yellow	**sarımtrak**	yellowish
kırmızı	red	**kırmızımtrak**	reddish
yeşil	green	**yeşilimtrak**	greenish
mor	purple	**morumtrak**	purplish
mavi	blue	**mavimtrak**	bluish
ekşi	sour	**ekşimtrak**	sourish
acı	bitter	**acımtrak**	bitterish

-(İ)MSİ

This suffix is added to nouns and adjectives to indicate that something

is 'almost of that kind or quality'. The first vowel is not used when the
suffix is added to words ending in a vowel; otherwise both vowels
harmonise with the preceding vowels. (For a similar suffix, see **-CE**:
section 137.)

acı	bitter	acımsı	bitterish, rather bitter
uzun	long	uzunumsu	longish, quite long
üzgün	sad	üzgünümsü	rather sad (not very sad but almost)
mavi	blue	mavimsi	bluish, almost blue

As you see in the above examples, the meaning of the suffix **-(İ)MSİ** is
rather like that of **-(İ)MTRAK**, but whereas **-(İ)MTRAK** is added to
words depicting colour and taste, **-(İ)MSİ** can be added to most nouns
or adjectives.

-CİK: diminutive

The suffix **-CİK** is added to nouns to express endearment, and
translates 'dear little ...', 'poor dear...'. It is also used with names as a
form of intimate address. It harmonises regularly with the base.

hayvan	animal	hayvancık	dear little animal
zavallı	helpless person	zavallıcık	poor helpless little person
kuzu	lamb	kuzucuk	dear little lamb
Ayşe		Ayşecik	dear little Ayşe

It is also quite usual to add the first person possessive suffix after **-CİK**,
especially with proper names or words indicating relationships between
people:

Ayşeciğim my dear little Ayşe, my dearest Ayşe
karı wife   **karıcığım** my dearest wife
koca husband   **kocacığım** my dearest husband
teyze aunt (maternal)   **teyzeciğim** my dearest auntie

The suffix **-CİK** can also be added to adjectives and adverbs and
intensifies the meaning of the word. When this suffix is added to
adjectives ending in **k**, the **k** is dropped:

küçük	small	küçücük	very small
yumuşak	soft	yumuşacık	very soft
sıcak	hot, warm	sıcacık	very warm
kısa	short	kısacık	very short

| yavaşça | slowly | yavaşçacık | very slowly |
| bu kadar | this much | bu kadarcık | only this much, just this much |

After some words, the -CİK suffix shows variations in form when used as an intensifier:

dar	narrow	daracık	very narrow, tight
az	little	azıcık	very little, just a bit
bir	one	biricik	one and only

Exercise 38

Translate into English:

1 Otelin adını ve adresini bilmiyorsanız nasıl bulacaksınız?
2 Türkçe konuşursak daha çabuk anlarlar.
3 İstediğim gün için uçakta yer bulabilirsem çok iyi olur.
4 Sizinle gelmemi isterseniz gelebilirim.
5 İyi değilsen doktor çağıralım.

Vocabulary

belli olmak	to become clear, obvious, certain
değişiklik	a change
bol bol	lots and lots, quite a lot
görüşmek	to meet up, discuss, get together

READING

Bir mektup

Sevgili Emel'ciğim,
    Sana şimdiye kadar yazamadığım için özür dilerim. Bu günlerde çok işimiz var. Her gün geç saatlere kadar çalışıp bitirmeye çalışıyoruz. Tatil programımız belli oldu. Eğer bir değişiklik olmazsa ben Temmuz'un altısında İstanbul'da olacağım. Ancak on gün kalabileceğim ama belki sonbaharda yine gelebilirim. Buradan istediğin bir şey varsa lütfen yaz, gelirken getiririm. Bavulumda çok yer var. İstanbul'dayken bir kaç gün için Şile'ye gidebilirsek çok iyi olur. Zeynepler de bu yaz orada olacaklarmış. Sen Şile'ye gitmek istemezsen belki başka bir yere

gidebiliriz, ama bunu ben oraya gelince konuşuruz. Bu mektup çok kısa oldu, ancak programımı sana hemen haber vermek istedim. İnşallah yakında bol bol görüşürüz.

Sevgiler,
İnci

Lesson 17

141 The passive

When the subject of a sentence does not perform the action indicated by the verb but is affected by that action, the passive form of the verb is used. The suffix which makes the verb passive comes before all other suffixes such as the negative, tense and person endings. The passive suffix has different forms depending on how the verb base ends:

a) If the verb base ends in a consonant other than **l**, the passive is formed by adding **-İL** to the verb base. Its variants are **-il, -ıl, -ül, -ul**:

sevmek	to love	**sevilmek**	to be loved
satmak	to sell	**satılmak**	to be sold
görmek	to see	**görülmek**	to be seen

b) If the verb base ends in **l**, then the passive is formed by adding **-İN** after this **l**; the vowel of this suffix harmonises with the base as usual, giving us the variants **-in, -ın, -ün, -un**:

bilmek	to know	**bilinmek**	to be known
almak	to take, buy	**alınmak**	to be taken, bought
bulmak	to find	**bulunmak**	to be found

c) If the verb base ends in a vowel, the passive is formed by adding just **-N** after that vowel:

okumak	to read	**okunmak**	to be read
kapamak	to close	**kapanmak**	to be closed
demek	to say, call	**denmek**	to be said, called

The object of the active sentence becomes the subject of the passive sentence and therefore drops the definite object ending that it may have:

active:	**Kapıyı açtı.**	He opened the door.
passive:	**Kapı açıldı.**	The door was opened.
	Gazeteyi okudum.	I read the newspaper.
	Gazete okundu.	The newspaper was read.

If the verb in the active sentence is intransitive (that is, if it is a verb that would not take an object), then the passive form of this verb cannot have a subject. It has what can be called an impersonal sense. This usually indicates a generalisation, and is used for translating active English sentences which have the words 'one' or 'people' as the subject:

Plaja nasıl gidilir? How does one get to the beach?
Türkiye'de 18 yaşında ehliyet alınır. One gets a driving licence at 18 in Turkey.
Her gece saat 11'de elektrikler söndürülür ve kapı kilitlenir. The lights are turned off and the door is locked at 11 every night.

Burada park yapılmaz.	No parking here.
Sigara içilmez.	No smoking.
Şoförle konuşulmaz.	One does not speak to the driver.

These last three examples with passive and negative forms convey the sense of 'it is forbidden to ...'. Such forms are used frequently on public notices.

The subject of an active sentence becomes the agent in a passive sentence, as in the following English examples:

'Ahmet opened the door'. Ahmet = subject; the door = object.
'The door was opened by Ahmet'. The door = subject; Ahmet = agent.

The agent in the English passive sentence is expressed in Turkish mostly by the word **taraf** followed by a possessive ending to indicate person, and that in turn is followed by the suffix **-dan**:
taraf + possessive + **dan**

The complete set of persons is as follows:

(benim) **tarafımdan**	by me
(senin) **tarafından**	by you
(onun) **tarafından**	by him/her/it
(bizim) **tarafımızdan**	by us
(sizin) **tarafınızdan**	by you
(onların) **tarafından**	by them
(or: **taraflarından**	if the personal pronoun is not used)

So the last example we had above, the English sentence 'The door was opened by Ahmet', is:

Kapı Ahmet tarafından açıldı.

Anlaşma bakanlar tarafından imzalandı. The agreement was signed by the ministers.
Bu fotoğraflar kimin tarafından çekildi? By whom were these pictures taken?
Ünlü yazar Steinbeck tarafından yazılan bütün eserler Türkçe'ye çevrildi. All the works written by the famous author Steinbeck have been translated into Turkish.

The agent in the passive sentence is sometimes formed by adding the suffix **-CE** to a noun. Those nouns that take the **-CE** suffix are essentially collective nouns, nouns that represent more than one person. Words like **hükümet** 'government', **halk** 'people, masses' can take the **-CE** suffix when they act as the agent in the sentence:

Hükümetçe yapılan açıklamada depremde evlerini kaybedenlere para yardımı yapılacağı belirtildi. In the statement made by the government, it was said that financial aid would be given to those who lost their homes in the earthquake.

Verbs that require certain suffixes like the dative **-(Y)E** or the ablative **-DEN** still require these in the passive:

Yılandan korkulur. One is scared of snakes.
Derse onda başlandı. The lesson was started at ten.

Certain verbs with the passive suffix can also be used as adjectives :

güvenmek to trust, rely on   **güvenilir** reliable
Ali çok güvenilir bir insandır. Ali is a very reliable man.
açılır kapanır something that can be a opened and closed
Yazın gelip kalan misafirler için açılır kapanır yatak aldım.
I bought a collapsible bed for the visitors who come and stay in the summer.

With negative verb stems:

inanılmaz bir hikaye	an unbelievable story
bulunmaz dost	a difficult-to-come-by friend
yenmez yemek	uneatable food
aşılmaz engel	an unsurmountable obstacle

Here are some further examples with the passive :

Türkiye'de bankalar saat kaçta açılıyor, kaçta kapanıyor?   At what time do the banks open and close in Turkey?

Almak istediğim halı çok fazla bir fiyata satılıyordu, onun için almadım. The carpet I wanted to buy was being sold for an excessive/ exorbitant price, so I did not buy it.
Bu yıl Türkiye'ye çok turist gelmesi bekleniyor. It is expected that a lot of tourists will come to Turkey this year.
Buna Türkçede ne denir? What is this called in Turkish?

Exercise 39

Translate into Turkish:
1 My friend's house has been sold.
2 The bag which was lost last week has been found.
3 A lot of tea is drunk in Turkey.
4 All the windows will be opened.
5 The letter written by him was read by everyone.

142 The reflexive

A reflexive verb indicates an action which the subject does to itself/himself, not to another person or thing. As the verbs that imply such an action are few, the reflexive suffix can be used with only a limited number of verbs. The reflexive suffix is **-(İ)N**; the vowel, if used, changes in accordance with the harmony rules.

yıkamak	to wash	**yıkanmak**	to wash oneself
giymek	to dress, put on	**giyinmek**	to dress oneself
övmek	to praise	**övünmek**	to praise oneself, to boast
taşımak	to carry	**taşınmak**	to move (as in moving house)
söylemek	to say, tell	**söylenmek**	to mutter (lit. say to oneself)

In the order in which suffixes are strung together, the reflexive comes before the passive. So a relexive sentence can be turned into a passive one, but not vice versa:

Kışın soğuk suyla yıkanılmaz. One does not wash (oneself) with cold water in the winter. (lit. One is not washed with cold water...)

143 The reflexive pronoun

The reflexive pronoun consists of the word **kendi** ('self') followed by the appropriate possessive suffix. As the reflexive pronoun refers to the subject, the possessive suffix that is added to **kendi** reflects the person of the subject.

kendim	myself
kendin	yourself
kendi or **kendisi**	himself, herself, itself
kendimiz	ourselves
kendiniz	yourselves
kendileri	themselves

There is virtually no difference in meaning between **kendi** and **kendisi**. In colloquial speech **kendi** is more frequently used. The reflexive pronoun can take all the suffixes that other pronouns take. Note that the third person singular **kendi** takes **n** before the case endings; the same happens with the third person plural, **kendileri**:

Yaşlı adam kendine rahat bir koltuk seçti. The old man chose a comfortable armchair for himself.

The reflexive pronoun can be used in any position in the sentence:

Bana bunu söyleyen kendisiydi. It was he himself who told me this.
Mektubu kendiniz mi yazdınız? Did you yourself write the letter?

The reflexive pronoun can be used to emphasise the subject:

Bunun yanlış olduğunu siz kendiniz söylediniz. You yourself said that this was wrong.
Onlar kendileri trenle gitmek istedi. They themselves wanted to go by train.

There can also be a repetition of **kendi** as:

kendi kendime	by myself, on my own
kendi kendine	by yourself
kendi kendine or **kendi kendisine**	by himself, etc.
kendi kendimize	by ourselves
kendi kendinize	by yourselves
kendi kendilerine	by themselves

As an adjective without any suffix **kendi** means 'own' :

Kendi işimi bitirdim, sana yardım edebilirim. I have finished my own task, I can help you.
Lütfen benim havlumu alma, kendi havlun nerede? Please do not take my towel, where is your own towel?

176

Vocabulary

başkent	capital	ülke ⎫	country
arasında	between	memleket ⎭	
görüşme	talks	sağlamak	to ensure, secure,
istek	request, wish		provide
ortaya koymak	to put forward,	çekici	attractive
	disclose,	alan	field
	declare	ortak	joint
mal	goods	proje	project
ihraç etmek	to export	durum	situation
ithal etmek	to import	güçleştirmek	to make
aynı şekilde	in the same way		something
artış	increase		difficult
ayrıca	also, besides	hükümet	government
şirket	firm, company	önlem	precaution,
yatırım	investment		measure

READING

İngiltere ile Türkiye'nin arasında Türkiye'nin başkenti Ankara'da dün başlayan görüşmeler devam ediyor. Özellikle ticaret ve turizm konularının görüşüldüğü toplantıda iki taraf isteklerini ortaya koydu. Türkiye İngiltere'ye daha çok mal ihraç etmek istiyor. Aynı şekilde İngiltere de Türkiye'ye sattığı mallarda artış bekliyor. Türkiye ayrıca yabancı şirketlerin ülkede yatırım yapmalarını sağlamaya çalışıyor. Turizm, yabancı şirketler için çekici olan bir yatırım alanı, ve bir çok ortak proje üzerinde çalışılıyor. Türkiye'de enflasyonun yüksek olması durumu güçleştiriyor, ancak hükümet tarafından alınan bazı önlemlerle bunun düşmesi bekleniyor.

Exercise 40

Translate into Turkish:
1 I washed and dressed in ten minutes.
2 I myself wanted to work in Istanbul.
3 You yourself (pl) wanted to stay here.
4 It is difficult to learn a foreign language by oneself.
5 Sitting by myself in front of the window, I watched those who passed by (lit. from) in the street.

Lesson 18

144 The causative

The causative form of a verb indicates that the subject is causing the action to happen rather than doing it directly, or is getting someone (or something) to do the action implied by the verb. The causative has different forms depending on the verb base it is used with:

a) The most widely used form of the causative is **-DİR**; the vowel of the suffix harmonises as usual. Although the causative form of each verb can be translated as 'to cause to...', there is usually a different word for these in English:

yemek	to eat	**yedirmek**	to feed (to cause to eat)
kesmek	to cut	**kestirmek**	to cause to cut
ölmek	to die	**öldürmek**	to kill
bilmek	to know	**bildirmek**	to announce, inform
yapmak	to do	**yaptırmak**	to cause to do, to get something done

b) If the verb base has more than one syllable and ends in a vowel or in the consonants **r** or **l**, the causative suffix is **-T**:

anlamak	to understand	**anlatmak**	to explain
hatırlamak	to remember	**hatırlatmak**	to remind
oturmak	to sit	**oturtmak**	to seat, to cause to sit
azalmak	to become less	**azaltmak**	to reduce, to cause to become less

c) A few verbs take the **-İT** form of the causative suffix:

korkmak	to fear	**korkutmak**	to frighten
akmak	to flow	**akıtmak**	to cause to flow, to pour

d) With a certain number of monosyllabic stems, the causative suffix is **-İR**; its variants are **-ir, -ır, -ür, -ur**;

düşmek	to fall	**düşürmek**	to drop
içmek	to drink	**içirmek**	to make drink
doğmak	to be born	**doğurmak**	to give birth to

177

Causative suffixes are frequently used to turn an intransitive verb (a verb that takes no object) into a transitive verb (which does take an object):

intrans.		*trans.*	
bitmek	to finish	**bitirmek**	to finish something
pişmek	to cook	**pişirmek**	to cook something
uçmak	to fly	**uçurmak**	to fly something
geçmek	to pass	**geçirmek**	to make something pass
durmak	to stop	**durdurmak**	to stop something

Ders bitti. The lesson ended.
Dersi bitirdim. I finished the lesson.
Ağrı geçti. The pain passed (went away).
Ağrıyı geçirdi. He made the pain pass (go away).
Otobüs durdu. The bus stopped
Otobüsü durdurdum. I stopped the bus.

e) The causative form is **-ER** or **-ERT** after a few transitive verbs; variants are **-er, -ar** or **-ert, -art**:

çökmek	to kneel, collapse	**çökertmek** to cause to kneel, collapse	
kopmak	to break off	**koparmak, kopartmak** to snap, break something	
çıkmak	to come out	**çıkarmak, çıkartmak** to take out, extract, subtract	
gitmek	to go	**gidermek** to remove, get rid of	

f) There are also some irregular causative forms:

görmek	to see	**göstermek**	to show (to make seen)
kalkmak	to get up	**kaldırmak**	to cause to get up, to lift, to remove

145 Uses of the causative

The causative has two basic meanings and is used accordingly:

1. The subject of the verb <u>causes</u> the action to happen.

a) In sentences where the basic verb is intransitive (i.e. has no direct object) and the causative suffix is used to turn the intransitive verb into a transitive verb, then the <u>subject</u> is the one that <u>performs</u> the action:

Adam öldü. The man died.
Adamı öldürdüm. I killed the man. (I caused the man to die.)
Tavuk pişti. The chicken is cooked.
Tavuğu pişirdim. I cooked the chicken.
Çocuk ağladı. The child cried.
Çocuğu ağlattım. I made the child cry.

Once an intransitive verb is turned into a transitive verb, as in the above sentences, a second causative suffix can then be added; this time to indicate that the <u>subject causes</u> the action to happen. This second causative is **-T** or **-DİR**. For example:

Et pişti. The meat is cooked.
Eti pişirdim. I cooked the meat.
Eti anneme pişirttim. I got my mother to cook the meat.

Cemal öldü. Cemal died.
Erol Cemal'i öldürdü. Erol killed Cemal.
Çetin, Cemal'i Erol'a öldürttü. Çetin got Erol to kill Cemal.

b) In sentences where the verb is already transitive and the subject is causing or getting an <u>agent</u> to do the action implied by the verb, this agent may or may not be specified:

Dişim çok ağrıyor, çektirmem lazım. My tooth is aching a lot, I have to have it extracted. (no agent mentioned)
Partiye gitmeden önce saçını yaptıracak mısın? Are you going to get your hair done before you go to the party? (no agent mentioned)
Lütfen bizi çok bekletmeyin. Please do not keep us waiting for long.

If the agent actually performing the action is mentioned in the sentence, then that agent takes the **-(Y)E** dative suffix:

Ali'ye ödevini yaptırdım. I made Ali do his homework.

(In this sentence <u>Ali</u> is the agent who is doing the homework, and <u>I</u> am the one who is causing/making him do it.)

Gözlüğüm yanımda olmadığı için mektubu arkadaşıma okuttum. As I did not have my glasses with me, I got my friend to read the letter.

2. A more restricted meaning of the causative is <u>allowing</u> an action to happen. In this case, the subject permits the action to take place.

Bütün gece çalan müzik beni uyutmadı. The music which played all night did not allow me to sleep.

Bize hiç bir şey söyletmediler. They did not let us say anything.

When a verb has two causatives (see p.179) and the first causative is **-İR** or **-DİR** then the second causative is **-T**:

bit-mek	**bit-ir-mek**	**bit-ir-t-mek**
çek-mek	**çek-tir-mek**	**çek-tir-t-mek**

If the first causative is **-T**, then the second causative is **-DİR**:

başla-mak	**başla-t-mak**	**başla-t-tır-mak**
temizle-mek	**temizle-t-mek**	**temizle-t-tir-mek**

As the causative suffix comes before the passive in the order of suffixation, causative verbs can be turned into passive but not vice versa:

Adam yılanı öldürdü. The man killed the snake.
Yılan adam tarafından öldürüldü. The snake was killed by the man.
Adam yılanı polise öldürttü. The man got the police to kill the snake.
Yılan adam tarafından polise öldürtüldü. The man had the snake killed by the police. (lit. the snake was killed by the police by the man)

Exercise 41

Translate into Turkish:
1 I got my friend to do this job.
2 The film made us laugh.
3 What made the pain go away? (lit. pass)
4 I got the guests' room cleaned very well; they may come this weekend.
5 His questions made the child cry.

146 The reciprocal

The reciprocal of the verb usually indicates that the action is mutually performed by two or more people. The reciprocal suffix is **-(İ)Ş**; its variants are **-ş** after vowels, and **-iş, -ış, -üş, -uş** after consonants.

181

dövmek	to beat	**dövüşmek**	to beat one another, to fight
anlamak	to understand	**anlaşmak**	to understand one another, to reach an agreement
bulmak	to find	**buluşmak**	to meet (find each other)
tanımak	to know, recognise	**tanışmak**	to be acquainted, to know each other
çarpmak	to strike, hit	**çarpışmak**	to collide
bakmak	to look	**bakışmak**	to gaze at each other

Another use of the reciprocal is to indicate action done together by several subjects:

gülmek	to laugh	**gülüşmek**	to laugh together
ağlamak	to cry	**ağlaşmak**	to cry together
bağırmak	to shout	**bağrışmak**	to shout together

Anlattığı hikayeyi dinlerken herkes gülüşüyordu. Everyone was laughing together while listening to the story that he was telling.
Sokakta bağrışan çocuklara susmalarını söyledim. I told the children who were shouting in the street to be quiet.

Yet another use of the reciprocal form is to indicate either that the action is being done by a number of subjects separately but with a common aim and in a repeated fashion, or by one subject repeatedly.

uçmak	to fly	**uçuşmak**	to fly about
koşmak	to run	**koşuşmak**	to run about

Kedinin yakaladığı kuşun tüyleri havada uçuşuyordu. The feathers of the bird that the cat caught were flying about in the air.
Tren kalkmak üzere olduğu için yetişmek isteyen herkes koşuşuyordu. As the train was about to leave, everyone who wanted to catch it was running about.
Tatile gitmeden önce hazırlıklarımı tamamlayabilmek için bütün gün koşuştum. I ran around all day in order to complete my preparations before going on holiday.

(In the last example, notice how the English word order is completely reversed in Turkish. You go to the end of the Turkish sentence and then start translating into English, working your way backwards.)

The reciprocal suffix is not used with many verbs because of the restrictions in meaning. Some verbs carrying this form have special meanings:

tutmak	to hold, catch	**tutuşmak**	to catch fire
tartmak	to weigh	**tartışmak**	to debate (lit. to weigh each other up)
yetmek	to suffice	**yetişmek**	to be brought up

Because of the mutual nature of the activity indicated by the verb, the reciprocal forms are generally used with **İLE/-(Y)LE** 'with, and':

Ayşe'yle Hasan bakıştılar. Ayşe and Hasan looked at each other.
Kamyon arabayla çarpıştığı halde yoluna devam etti. Although the lorry collided with the car, it continued on its way.
Kiminle buluşuyorsun? Whom are you meeting (with)?

A verb cannot take both the reciprocal and the reflexive suffixes together at the same time. The reciprocal suffix comes before the causative and the passive suffixes, which means that reciprocal verbs can be made causative or passive or both:

Partide herkesle tanıştırıldım. I was introduced to everyone at the party.

Causative and passive verbs cannot be turned into the reciprocal form.

147 The reciprocal pronoun

The reciprocal pronoun **birbiri** means 'each other'. It brings in the sense of mutual activity to the sentence if the verb is not reciprocal. It cannot stand as the subject of the sentence:

birbirimiz	each other of us (one another of us)
birbiriniz	each other of you
birbiri/birbirleri	each other of them

Durumu anladık, ancak birbirimize birşey söylemedik. We realised the situation, but did not say anything to each other.
Birbirinizin kitabını kullanmayın, kendi kitabınızı kullanın. Do not use each other's book(s), use your own book(s).

When it is formed with the third person possessive suffix, it takes an **n** before the case endings:
Çocuklar birbirlerine şeker verdiler. The children gave each other sweets.

Vocabulary

kamyon	lorry	**yük**	load
yön	direction	**yüklü**	loaded
korkunç	awful, terrible, horrible	**olay yeri**	place or scene of incident
yaralanmak	to be injured	**hayat** ⎫	life
ağır	(in this context) seriously	**yaşam** ⎭	
		devlet	state
plaka	number plate	**devlet hastanesi**	state hospital
sollamak	to overtake on the left	**hatalı**	wrong
		aşırı	excessive
bu arada	meanwhile, in the meantime	**hız**	speed
		yüzünden	because of
viraj	bend	**meydana gelmek**	to happen, to come about
araç	vehicle		
birdenbire	suddenly	**karayolu**	highway

READING

Bir Gazeteden

Amasya'dan Samsun'a gitmekte olan bir yolcu otobüsü ile karşı yönden gelen bir kamyon Samsun yakınlarında çarpıştı. Korkunç kazada on beş kişi öldü, yedi kişi ağır yaralandı.

05 AT 318 plakalı kamyon Samsun'a otuz beş kilometre kala önündeki bir başka kamyonu sollamak istedi. Bu arada bir viraja girmiş olan araçların karşısına birdenbire 34 N 3217 plakalı yolcu otobüsü çıktı. Kum yüklü kamyon ile karşı yönden gelen otobüs büyük bir hızla çarpıştı. Otuz yedi yolcusu olan otobüste onbeş kişi olay yerinde hayatını kaybetti. Kamyon ve otobüsün şoförleri ölenler arasında. Yaralılar Samsun Devlet Hastanesine kaldırıldı. Dikkatsizlik, hatalı sollama ve aşırı hız yüzünden meydana gelen kazadan sonra Samsun – Ankara karayolu dört saat trafiğe kapatıldı.

Key

LESSON 1

Exercise 2: otelde, arabada, uçakta, otobüste, trende, çayda, kahvede, halıda, şarapta

Exercise 3: şekerli, limonlu, tuzlu, biberli, etli, kokulu, paralı, telefonlu, numaralı, kumlu

LESSON 2

Exercise 4: 1 short hair 2 a young lawyer 3 a red coat 4 blue eyes 5 big hotels 6 small houses 7 I am Turkish, you are British. 8 The woman is ill. 9 You are lazy. 10 The small children are tired.

Conversation
- Good morning.
- Good morning.
- How are you?
- I'm well, thank you. How are you?
- I also am well, thank you.
- This morning the sea is very nice.
- Yes, but isn't it cold?
- No, it isn't cold, but the weather is cold.
- Yes. Goodbye.
- Goodbye.

Exercise 5A: 1 The young woman is not tired. 2 Is the big hotel cheap? 3 How is the weather, is it cold? 4 Who is the man? 5 Is the carpet blue or green? 6 Isn't the black car new? 7 The door is closed, but the window is open. **B:** 1 Genç adam polis değil. 2 Ev ne renk? 3 Kırmızı ve mavi halı büyük ve güzel, ama pahalı da. 4 Oda küçük değil mi? 5 Nasılsınız? 6 Yaşlı adam nasıl, iyi mi? 7 Yeşil ve sarı renkler güzel.

LESSON 3

Exercise 6A: 1 There are two windows, one door, one large table, five chairs and an armchair in this room. 2 There are two green cushions in the brown armchair. 3 What colour carpet is there on the floor? 4 Who is in the garden? 5 Isn't there a cupboard in the room? 6 There is no curtain on the window. 7 There is (are) guest(s) in the house. **B:** 1 Masada kitaplar, kalemler ve defterler var. 2 Bende para yok. 3 Küçük bahçede hayvan yok. 4 Sokakta bir araba yok mu? 5 Odada duvarlar ve perdeler ne renk? 6 Ağır kutuda ne var? 7 Sinemada iyi bir film var mı?

Conversation
- Good morning. Yes sir/madam.
- Good morning. Are there (any) grapes?
- There are (yes) sir.
- A kilo please.
- OK.
- How much?
- A kilo, eight hundred and fifty lira.
- Here you are, thank you.
- Good day.
- Good day.

Exercise 7A: 1 Today the weather is not cold, but it is rainy. 2 Two rooms with bath please. 3 Is there (any) chocolate ice-cream? 4 How many roomed is this house? (i.e. How many rooms does this house have?) 5 There are three children in the street with blue coat(s). **B:** 1 Bir sütlü kahve lütfen. 2 Ben Ankaralı değilim, Londralıyım. 3 Resimli kitap nerede? 4 Banyolu oda kaç para? (*or:* ne kadar?) 5 Mavi halı küçük ama pahalı.

LESSON 4

Exercise 8A: 1 I stayed in Istanbul for fifteen days. 2 I worked for two hours. 3 In Bodrum I swam in the sea and sat on the beach. 4 We had a nice meal and drank wine. 5 I sat in the room and wrote letter(s). **B:** 1 İki kitap okudum. 2 Çalıştı. 3 Dün çok yüzdük. 4 Çocuk evde kaldı. 5 Siz anladınız.

Exercise 9: 1 Bir otelde kalmadım. 2 Anlamadı. 3 Başlamadı. 4 Siz görmediniz. 5 Plajda oturmadılar.

Exercise 10: 1 (a) Evet, elma yedik. (b) Hayır, elma yemedik. 2 (a) Evet, otelde çay içtik. (b) Hayır, otelde çay içmedik. 3 (a) Evet, gazete aldım. (b) Hayır, gazete almadım. 4 (a) Evet, sinemada uyudun. (b) Hayır, sinemada uyumadın. 5 (a) Evet, çok çalıştınız. (b) Hayır, çok çalışmadınız.

Exercise 11A: 1 I opened the cupboard and took the big bag.
2 Who did this? 3 I did not see the table. 4 The weather is very bad,
the planes did not take off. 5 I turned the radio on, and turned the TV
off. **B:** 1 Arabayı sokakta bıraktım. 2 Elmayı yedin mi? 3 Ona
postaneyi göstermedim. 4 Londra'yı görmedim. 5 Bunu anladınız mı?

Reading: Yesterday morning I got up late, I didn't go to work; I went
to the shops; I did shopping. I bought a large white bag, then I went
back home. I ate bread, cheese, fruit. I watched a good film on television
and went to bed. I read (a book) in bed, then I slept.

Exercise 12: 1 I took the child to the hospital. 2 He closed the
windows, opened the door. 3 We had tea with milk. They ate fruit-
flavoured ice-cream. 4 I gave Ayşe the red bag, and she gave me this
book. 5 Whom did you ring? 6 I didn't put the heavy books on the
table, I put them on the floor.

LESSON 5

Exercise 13: 1 This morning a lot of cars went by the house. 2 We
didn't swim at the hotel beach. 3 The inside of the white cupboards is
not empty. 4 The young friend of the old man took him to the station.
5 What is there opposite your hotel? 6 Evin arkasında bahçe yok.
7 Eczanenin içinde sigara içmedik. 8 Sabun ve havlular dolabın içinde.
9 Odamızda sıcak su yok. 10 Bodrum'da hangi otelde kaldınız?

Exercise 14: 1 I closed the door of the bedroom. 2 All of these cups
are nice; which one have you bought? 3 Our hotel does not have any
rooms without bath. 4 Polis arabasını görmedim. 5 Misafirleriniz
nerede? Gelmediler mi? 6 Kaç çocuğunuz var? 7 Bu ceketlerin hepsi
güzel, ama beyazı çok pahalı.

Conversation
– What did you do yesterday?
– We went to the museum. We saw very interesting things in the
museum.
– Is the museum large?
– No, it's not very big; we saw all of it in two hours. There's a small
shop beside (next to) the museum. My friends bought souvenirs from
there, but I didn't buy (any), because I didn't have much money.
– Where did you have lunch (eat meal)?

- We found a restaurant behind the museum. Its food is quite (very) delicious. Well, what did you do?
- We went in the sea, sat on the sand and sunbathed.
- Very nice.

LESSON 6

Exercise 15: 1 That's a very nice place; thirty people came from London and stayed there for fifteen days. 2 The car didn't go forwards, it went backwards. 3 What is this the key of? 4 I was very ill on Friday, I went to the doctor. 5 I rang you yesterday evening, you weren't in your room. 6 Çok hızlı konuştu, anlamadım. 7 Burası çok güzel bir yer. 8 Burada kaç kişi kaldı? 9 Otobüs burada durdu mu? 10 İstanbul'da hava hergün çok sıcaktı.

Exercise 16: 1 Geçen yıl Türkiye'de değildik. 2 Öğleyin dükkanlar kapalı değil, ama bankalar kapalı. 3 Cuma akşamları sinemaya gideriz. 4 Perşembe günü neredeydiniz? 5 Kitabın hepsini okudum.

Reading: Last month we went to Marmaris. Our hotel was on the sea shore. The hotel had a large garden and a wide beach. The beach was very nice. The food in (of) the hotel was also very nice; the waiters and the service were very good. There was a bath or a shower in each room. Some evenings we turned the radio on and listened to music. There was a small island opposite our hotel; one day we went to that island and we went in the sea there. We stayed in Marmaris for fifteen days and had a very nice holiday.

LESSON 7

Reading: I get up early in the mornings. I go into the bathroom, and I wash my face, comb my hair and put on my dress/suit. I always drink tea at breakfast; I like tea very much and drink (it) without milk. I eat a slice of toast and cheese; I do not eat butter or jam. At eight I leave (go out of) the house, I walk to the bus stop. I go to my work by bus. What do you eat for breakfast? How do you go to work?

Exercise 17: 1 Bu yıl Türkiye'ye gidiyoruz. 2 İstasyona yürümüyorum, otobüse biniyorum. 3 Türkçe bilmiyoruz, ama öğreniyoruz. 4 Bizimle geliyor musunuz? 5 Çocuklar havuzda yüzüyorlardı.

Exercise 18: 1 Birinci otobüs doluydu, onun için ikinci otobüse bindik. 2 İkişer bardak çay içtik. 3 Geçen Pazardan beri bu otelde kalıyoruz. 4 Otele kadar yürüdüm. 5 Yemekten sonra ne yaptınız?

Conversation: On the phone

- Hello Ayşe, is that you?
- Hello Ahmet, how are you?
- Very well, thank you. How are you?
- I too am well.
- Ayşe, tomorrow we're going on a boat trip. You're coming, aren't you?
- Of course I'm coming. But what time does the boat leave?
- It leaves from in front of the Büyük Hotel at ten in the morning. After having lunch in a small cove, we stay in this cove for about three hours, and go in the sea. After having our tea there as well, we go back to the Büyük Hotel.
- Are Serpil and Cengiz coming too?
- Of course.
- OK, where do we meet?
- We meet at the hotel at nine o'clock and have breakfast first.
- All right, I'll also be there at nine.
- OK. Goodbye.
- Goodbye.

Exercise 19: 1 Eylül'e kadar tatildeyiz. 2 Uçak kalkmadan önce biletimi kaybettim, ama sonra buldum. 3 Sigara içmeden önce bütün pencereleri açtık. 4 Dün gece, siz gittikten sonra, Londra'ya telefon ettim.

LESSON 8

Exercise 20: 1 Lütfen sigara içmeyiniz. 2 Kapıyı kapayın lütfen. 3 Onları bekleyelim. 4 Bavullarımız ağır, onun için otele taksiyle gidelim. 5 Masanın üstündeki kitaplar benim.

Reading: Next week I shall go to Ankara for a meeting. After staying in Ankara for three days, I shall go (pass) on to Izmir by plane. We are setting up a large factory in Izmir. This factory will be like the factories in Britain. The number of workers in the factory is about 850. We shall send some of these workers to Britain for a period of three months each. In this way they will learn a little bit of English. After talking to the manager of the factory and others, I shall return to London. I shall write a short report about my trip.

Exercise 21: 1 Yeni bir araba alacağım. 2 Yarın gelecek misiniz? 3 Su içmeyecek.

LESSON 9

Exercise 22: 1 Soğuk bir bira ister misiniz? 2 Otobüs İzmir'den Kuşadası'na iki saatte gider. 3 Müzeye girer girmez onu gördüm. 4 Türkiye'deyken Türkçe konuştuk. 5 Odadan çıkarken kapıyı kapattı. **Exercise 23:** 1 Saat yarımda buluşalım. 2 Uçak Dalaman'dan üçe on kala kalkıyor: biz saat bir buçukta havaalanında olacağız. 3 Ankara'ya trenle sekiz saatte gittik. 4 Gümrükten geçerken bavullarımızı açmadılar.

Reading: We go to Turkey every year for (our) holiday and stay three weeks. Generally we go at the end of May or in September. We do not go in the summer months, because the weather is very hot. Each year we stay in a different hotel and thus see different places. The hotels arrange tours to historical places nearby. When going with these tours, we see a lot of things without getting tired. When coming back we stay in Istanbul for a few days. Istanbul is a different city: it is crowded, noisy, and transport is difficult, but I like Istanbul very much. It is not like European cities. In Istanbul we do a little shopping. We buy small presents for our friends. The three-week holiday goes very quickly. While going to the airport by taxi, we think of our next year's holiday.

LESSON 10

Exercise 24: 1 En pahalı otel en iyi otel değil. 2 İstanbul Londra'dan sıcak. 3 Odamız oteldeki en küçük oda. 4 Uçak çok geç gelmiş. 5 İki yıl önce İstanbul'a gitmiştim, ama bu müzeyi görmemiştim.

Exercise 25: 1 Antalya'da hava çok soğukmuş. 2 Ayşe'ye telefon ettim, ama evde yokmuş. 3 Orada iki hafta kalacakmış. 4 Süt çok besleyiciymiş. 5 Yolcular uçağı üç saatten beri bekliyorlarmış.

Conversation: At the reception
– Good day.
– Good day. Can I help you, sir?
– Do you have (a) vacant room?
– For tonight?
– Yes.
– A room for how many people?
– For two people, please.
– How long will you be staying?
– Three days for the moment.
– Unfortunately we don't have a room for three nights, but we have a

nice room with bath for two nights. Let us give you another room for
the third night.
- Are these rooms overlooking the sea?
- The first room overlooks the garden, the second room overlooks the
sea.
- Is the side overlooking the garden noisy?
- No. Our garden is very big, the approach road of the hotel is far away
from the building. Our rooms overlooking the garden are cheaper.
- How much is it per night?
- Ninety thousand lira for two people. The rooms on the sea side are
one hundred and ten thousand lira per night. That's including VAT.
- Is breakfast included?
- No, breakfast is extra (not included). Breakfast is two thousand five
hundred lira per person.
- OK, let's stay here for three days.
- Can you give me your passport or identity please?
- Here you are.
- Thanks.

LESSON 11

Exercise 26: 1 Ne çay ne kahve içiyorum; meyve suyu seviyorum.
2 Evinin bahçesi hem büyük, hem güneşli. 3 Pencereyi açarken lütfen
kapıyı kapatır mısınız? 4 Mayomuzu giyerek plaja gittik. 5 Evde kalıp
bizi bekleyeceksiniz. 6 Bütün gün çalışa çalışa yoruldum. 7 Bizi
beklemeden gittiler. 8 Buraya geleli onu görmüyorum. 9 Güneşte
oturmaktansa, denize girelim. 10 Bu resimlere baktıkça mutlu
oluyorum.

LESSON 12

Exercise 27: 1 Burada kalmak istemiyorum. 2 Pul almak için nereye
gittin? 3 Beşten önce bizi aramağa çalışacak. 4 Otelde olmasını rica
ettik. 5 Bunu bana söylemene rağmen, anlamadım.

Exercise 28: 1 Bu yastık bana lazım değil, ister misin? 2 Dokuz
buçukta orada olmak için erken kalkmamız lazım. 3 Türk arkadaşlarınla
konuşmak için Türkçe öğrenmen lazım. 4 Gece saat on ikiden sonra
radyoyu açmamalısın. 5 Ona biraz para vermem lazım.

Reading: When you go on holiday during the summer months, you
have (i.e. one has) to pay attention to a number of things. In particular,
you must not sit in the sun for a long time. In the middle of the day (lit.

during the midday hours) the sun's rays are very strong and burning, so you have to be careful when sunbathing. The most suitable times for sunbathing are before twelve and after half past three. So as not to get too burnt in the sun, you should apply protective cream. Also you must drink plenty of water, as the body loses water. It is dangerous to eat a lot and drink alcohol at lunch and then to go in the sea. If you follow this advice (lit. these), you will have a pleasant, comfortable holiday.

LESSON 13

Exercise 29: 1 Dalaman'a giden uçak dolu. 2 Burada duran otobüsler Efes'e gidiyor. 3 Burada kalmış olanlar yine gelmek istiyorlar. 4 Yarın bizi görecek vakti yokmuş. 5 Seninkine benzer (benzeyen) bir çanta istiyorum.

Exercise 30: 1 Evi Kaş'ta olan arkadaşımız İngiltere'ye gelmek istiyor. 2 Bavulları daha otelde olan yolcular havaalanına gitmek için otobüse biniyorlar. 3 Pencereleri kapalı olan oda çok havasız. 4 Yemekleri çok lezzetli olan bir otelde kaldık. 5 Cepleri olmayan bu ceketi sevmiyorum.

Conversation

- Excuse me, where does the bus going to Ankara leave from?
- Within one hour there are two buses to Ankara, one via Bursa and one via Bolu. Which is yours?
- Mine's the one via Bolu.
- The bus that goes (lit. will go) via Bolu leaves from beside that building. It will arrive before long (lit. a little afterwards).
- Thank you.

Exercise 31: 1 Fincanları kuruladıktan sonra pencerenin yanındaki dolabın içine koydum. 2 Bavulunu hazırladın mı? 3 Yirmi seneden beri Türkiye dışında oturmana rağmen, yabancılaşmadın. 4 Güneşte yanmış olanlar daha güzelleşti. 5 Sorumu tekrarlamamı istedi/rica etti.

LESSON 14

Exercise 32: 1 Evin önünde gördüğüm adam hırsızdı. 2 Lokantada yediğimiz yemek pahalı değildi. 3 Şimdi okuduğun kitabı ben de okudum. 4 Kalacağın otelin ismini biliyor musun? 5 Seyredeceğimiz film Türkiye'de çalışan İngilizleri gösteriyor.

Exercise 33: 1 I don't know the name of the man I bought a coffee for, but you know him very well. 2 There was no food in the saucepan

I put the lid on. 3 There were no tickets left for the concert we wanted to go to. 4 Where is the woman whose suitcase you carried/are carrying going? 5 You will give the paper you are filling in to the customs officer. 6 Adını unuttuğum kadın bana bu bakır tepsiyi verdi. 7 Yirmi dakika geciktiğimi söyledi. 8 Gümrük memuru bavulumu açmamı istedi. 9 Burada olduğumu bilmiyordu. 10 Türk Havayollarıyla geleceklerini söylediler. İngiliz Havayolları uçakları doluymuş.

Conversation: At the customs
- Your passport please.
- Here you are.
- How long will you stay in Turkey?
- About three weeks.
- Which cases are yours?
- This black case.
- Have you got anything you have to pay duty on?
- I don't think so.
- Have you any electrical goods?
- No.
- Would you open your case, please?
- OK, one minute please, I'll just find the key . . . Here you are, look.
- What a lot of shirts (you have) here . . . There are rather too many for three weeks, aren't there? And what's more, these are still in their packaging.
- As I'll be staying for three weeks, it'll just be enough. And I'll give three or four of them to the friend in whose house I'll be staying.
- These are all the same size.
- I asked my friend. According to what he wrote in (his) letter, we take (lit. put on) the same size. I've also bought this doll for my friend's daughter. It's her birthday next week - she'll be six years old.
- Have you any presents other than the ones you've mentioned?
- No, that's all.
- OK, go ahead, carry on. Have a good holiday.
- Thank you.

Exercise 34: 1 Kaldığımız otel beklediğimiz kadar rahat değildi. 2 Bildiğiniz gibi bu eve geçen sene taşındık. 3 Arkadaşımın söylediğine göre Türkiye'de enflasyon yüksekmiş. 4 Mağazada, aldığımdan başka iki ceket daha vardı. 5 Gelmediğiniz takdirde biletleri ona veririm.

LESSON 15

Exercise 35: 1 Havaalanına gelme, uçak gecikebilir. Bir taksiye bineriz. 2 On dakika bekleyebilir misiniz? 3 Size bir şey sorabilir miyim? 4 Gazeteye baktım, fakat o haberi göremedim/bulamadım. 5 Saat altıdan önce telefon etme; evde olmayabilir.

Reading: When you go into a mosque in Turkey, you have to take off your shoes before entering. Because mosques are places of worship, you cannot wander around inside as you wish. Women must cover their heads. It is possible you may not have with you a scarf or something else to cover your head. In that case, you'll be able to ask for a headscarf from one of the officials there, and when you go out of the mosque you'll give it back. You must not speak in a loud voice in the mosque. You may need to get permission to take photographs. Entry to mosques is free. In some mosques there is a box for donations; those who wish can put (lit. throw) money into it.

Exercise 36: 1 Okulda Fransızca öğrendim ama iyi konuşamıyorum. 2 Sizce bu doğru mu? 3 Hollandalı arkadaşlarımız Türkçe öğrenmek istiyor. 4 İngilizce öğrenmek istediğiniz için İngiltere'ye gelmelisiniz. 5 Yer bulamadıkları için oturamadılar.

LESSON 16

Exercise 37: 1 Telefon etse gelmesini söylerim. 2 Mektubunuzu alsam cevap verirdim. 3 Yorgunsan sinemaya gelme. 4 Burada kalmayacaksanız nerede kalacaksınız? 5 Çok çalışırsam zengin olacağım.

Exercise 38: 1 If you do not know the name and the address of the hotel, how will you find it? 2 If we speak in Turkish they'll understand more quickly. 3 If I can find a seat on the plane for the day I want, it would be very good. 4 If you would like me to come with you I can come. 5 If you are not well let's call a doctor.

Reading: A letter
My dearest Emel,
I am sorry I have not been able to write to you until now. These days we have a lot of work. Every day we work till late and try and finish it. Our holiday programme is clear. If there is no change I shall be in Istanbul on 6th July. I shall be able to stay only ten days, but perhaps I can come again in the autumn. If there is anything you want from here

please write, and I'll bring it when I come. There is plenty of space in my suitcase. It would be very good (nice) if we can go to Şile for a few days while in Istanbul. Apparently Zeynep and her family will also be there this summer. If you wouldn't want to go to Şile perhaps we can go somewhere else, but we'll discuss (talk about) this when I come over there. This letter has been very short, but I wanted to let you know (to inform you of) my programme at once. Hope we'll see each other a lot soon.

Love
İnci

LESSON 17

Exercise 39: 1 Arkadaşımın evi satıldı. 2 Geçen hafta kaybolan çanta bulundu. 3 Türkiye'de çok çay içilir (içiliyor). 4 Bütün pencereler açılacak. 5 Onun tarafından yazılan mektup herkes tarafından okundu.

Reading: The talks between Britain and Turkey which started yesterday in Ankara, the capital of Turkey, are going on (continuing). In the meeting where especially the subjects (issues) of trade and tourism were discussed, the two sides put forward their requests. Turkey wants to export more goods to Britain. In the same way, Britain also expects an increase in the goods that she sells to Turkey. Besides that, Turkey is trying to secure foreign firms' making investments in the country. Tourism is an attractive area of investment for foreign companies, and they are working on many joint projects (lit. many joint projects are being worked on). The inflation being high in Turkey makes the situation more difficult, but it is expected that this will fall through (by means of) various measures taken by the government.

Exercise 40: 1 On dakikada yıkandım ve giyindim. 2 Ben kendim İstanbul'da çalışmak istedim. 3 Siz kendiniz burada kalmak istediniz. 4 Kendi kendine yabancı bir dil öğrenmek zor. 5 Pencerenin önünde kendi kendime oturarak sokaktan geçenleri seyrettim.

LESSON 18

Exercise 41: 1 Bu işi arkadaşıma yaptırdım. 2 Film bizi güldürdü. 3 Ağrıyı ne geçirdi? 4 Misafirlerin odasını çok iyi temizlettim; bu hafta sonu gelebilirler. 5 Soruları çocuğu ağlattı.

Reading: From a newspaper
A (passenger) coach travelling from Amasya to Samsun and a lorry
coming from the opposite direction crashed into each other (collided)
near Samsun. In the terrible accident fifteen people died and seven
people were seriously injured.

The lorry with the number plate 05 AT 318 tried (wanted) to overtake
another lorry in front of it thirty five kilometres from Samsun. The
vehicles which had by then (meanwhile) entered a bend were suddenly
confronted by the coach with the number plate 34 N 3217. The lorry
which was loaded with sand and the coach coming from the opposite
direction collided at great speed. In the coach, which had thirty seven
passengers, fifteen people died at the scene of the incident (accident).
The drivers of the lorry and the coach are amongst those who died. The
injured were taken to Samsun State Hospital. After the accident, which
happened because of carelessness, wrong overtaking and excessive
speed, the Samsun - Ankara highway was closed to traffic for four
hours.

Mini-dictionary

For numbers see sections 24, 64, 65, for days of the week section 55, for the names of the months section 56 and for seasons section 57.

a, an bir
about hakkında, kadar
above üst
across karşı
address adres
aeroplane uçak
afraid of, be kork
after sonra
afternoon öğleden sonra
again bir daha, yine
agreement anlaşma
air hava
airport havaalanı
all of it/them hepsi
always her zaman
and ve
angry, be kız
animal hayvan
answer (n) cevap, yanıt
answer (v) cevapla, yanıtla
antique antika
apple elma
appointment randevu
approach (v) yaklaş
approximately aşağı yukarı,
  yaklaşık
armchair koltuk
arrive var
as gibi
ask sor
attention dikkat
author yazar

back, behind arka
backward geri
bad kötü, fena
bag çanta
bank banka
bath banyo
bathing suit mayo
bathroom banyo

bay koy
be ol
beach plaj
beautiful güzel
become ol
become tired yorul
because çünkü
bed yatak
bedroom yatak odası
bee arı
before önce
begin başla
believe inan
bell (door) zil
beside yan
big büyük
bill hesap
birthday doğum günü
bite (v) ısır
bitter acı
black siyah
Black Sea Karadeniz
blood kan
blue mavi
boil kayna
book kitap
born, be doğ
bottle şişe
bottom alt
box kutu
boy oğlan
brake (v) kır
bread ekmek
breakfast kahvaltı
bring (along) getir
brown kahverengi
bucket kova
building bina
burn (v) yan
burst (v) patla
bury göm

196

bus otobüs
bus stop durak
busy meşgul
but ama, ancak, fakat
buy al, satın al

call (v) çağır
candle mum
capital başkent, başşehir
car araba
car park otopark
carpet halı
carry taşı
cat kedi
catch (v) yakala
cause sebep, neden
ceiling tavan
chair iskemle, sandalye
change (something) (v) değiştir
cheap ucuz
cheese peynir
chemist eczane
cheque çek
chicken tavuk
child çocuk
chocolate çikolata
choose seçmek
cigarette sigara
cinema sinema
city kent, şehir
classroom sınıf
clean temiz
cleaner (n) temizleyici
clever akıllı
clock saat
close (v) kapa
closed kapalı
cloth (cover) örtü
coat palto
coffee kahve
cold (adj) soğuk
cold, be üşü
collapse (v) çök
collect topla
collide çarpış
colour renk
come gel
come out, leave çık
come to an end bit

comfortable rahat
complain şikayet et
complaint şikayet
concerning hakkında
concert konser
continually sürekli
cook (n) ahçı
cook (v intransitive) pişir
cook (v transitive) piş
cool serin
corner köşe
correct(ly) doğru
cough (v) öksür
country ülke, memleket
cover (v) ört
crash çarp
cross (v) geç
crowded kalabalık
cup fincan
cupboard dolap
curtain perde
cushion yastık
customer müşteri
customs gümrük
cut (v) kes

daily günlük
day gün
deep derin
delay (n) gecikme
delayed, be gecik
dentist dişçi
depart (of planes, trains etc.) kalk
dial (v) çevir
die öl
diet (n) rejim
different değişik
dinner yemek, akşam yemeği
divide (v) böl
do yap
doctor doktor
dog köpek
door kapı
downward aşağı
dream rüya, düş
dress elbise
drink (alcoholic) (n) içki
drink (v) iç
drive (v) sür, kullan

driver şoför
drop (v) düşür
dry (adj) kuru
dry (v) kurula
dust toz

early erken
earn kazan
ear-ring küpe
earthquake deprem
eat ye
empty boş
end (n) son
end, come to an bit
engineer mühendis
English (person) İngiliz
enough yeter, kafi
enter gir
entrance giriş
Europe Avrupa
evening akşam
every her
exact(ly) tam
excessive fazla
excluded hariç
exit çıkış
expect bekle
expenditure gider
expensive pahalı
explain anlat
exterior dış
eye göz

face yüz
fast (adv) çabuk
fat şişman
father baba
fear korku
feel (v) hisset, duy
female kadın
film film
find (v) bul
finish (v transitive) bitir
first ilk
fish balık
flat (n) daire, kat
floor yer
flower çiçek
foot ayak

for için
foreign(er) yabancı
forget (v) unut
forgive affet
forward ileri
free (not occupied) boş, serbest
free (without charge) bedava,
  parasız
fresh taze
friend arkadaş
front ön
fruit meyve
full dolu
full (replete) tok
furniture eşya
future gelecek

garden bahçe
get al
get on bin
get up kalk
girl kız
give ver
glass bardak
go git
go in, enter gir
go out (of lights, fire) sön
go shopping alışverişe çık/git ,
  çarşıya çık
go to bed yat
good iyi
grape üzüm
grass çimen
green yeşil
ground yer
guest misafir

hair saç
half yarım, buçuk
hand el
hand luggage el bagajı
hang as
hanger askı
happy mutlu
hard-working çalışkan
hat şapka
headline başlık
health sağlık
hear duy

heat ısı, sıcaklık
heavy ağır
help (v) yardım et
hit (v) vur
hold (v) tut
holiday tatil
homework ödev
honey bal
hope (n) umut, ümit
hope (v) um, ümit et
horse at
hospital hastane
hot (of taste) acı
hot (of temperature) sıcak
hotel otel
hour saat
house ev
how nasıl
how many kaç
how much ne kadar
hungry aç
husband koca

ice buz
ice-cream dondurma
identity kimlik
ill hasta
included dahil
income gelir
inside, interior iç
interesting ilginç
interfere karış
invention buluş
inward içeri
island ada

jacket ceket
journey yolculuk, gezi, seyahat
just ancak

key anahtar
kill (v) öldür
know (a fact etc.) bil
know (a person) tanı

ladder merdiven
lake göl
lamb kuzu
lamp lamba

land (of aircraft) (v) in
language dil
large büyük
late geç
later sonra
laugh (n) gülüş
laugh (v) gül
laundry çamaşır
lawyer avukat
lazy tembel
lean out sark
learn öğren
leave (v) bırak, ayrıl
left sol
lemon limon
lesson ders
letter mektup
lid kapa
lie (n) yalan
lie (v) yalan söyle
lie down yat
life hayat, yaşam
light (n) ışık
light (in colour) açık
light (in weight) hafif
like, approve of beğen
listen dinle
a little az
live (v) yaşa
live (reside) otur
lively canlı
load yük
long uzun
look (v) bak
look for ara
look like benze
lose kaybet
lost kayıp
lost, be kaybol
love, like (v) sev

machine makine
make (v) yap
make a noise gürültü yap
male erkek
man adam
many çok, bir çok
market çarşı, pazar
meal yemek

meat et
medicine ilaç
Mediterranean Akdeniz
meet up buluş
meeting toplantı
message mesaj
milk süt
miss, yearn for özle
mistake yanlış
money para
month ay
moon ay
more daha
morning sabah
most en
mother anne, ana
mountain dağ
much çok
museum müze
music müzik

narrow dar
nation ulus, millet
necessary gerek, lazım
new yeni
news haber
newspaper gazete
next gelecek
night gece
noise gürültü
noise, make a gürültü yap
noon öğle
not değil
notebook defter
nourishing besleyici
now şimdi
number numara, sayı

office daire
old eski yaşlı, ihtiyar
only ancak, yanlız
open (adj) açık
open (v) aç
opposite karşı
or veya, ya da
order, command (v) emret
outside dış
outward dışarı

pain acı, ağrı
palace saray
paper kağıt
parcel paket
park park
party parti
pass (v) geç
passenger yolcu
past geçmiş
path yol
pay (v) öde
pay attention dikkat et
peach şeftali
pear armut
pen, pencil kalem
pepper biber
person, people kişi
personal kişisel
petrol benzin
photograph fotoğraf
picnic piknik
picture resim
piece parça
pink pembe
place (n) yer
place (v) koy
plate tabak
play (v) oyna
pleasant hoş
please lütfen
please (v) memnun et
pleased, be (v) memnun ol
pocket cep
police/policeman polis
pool havuz
poor fakir, yoksul
post office postane
prefer tercih et
prepare hazırla
present hediye, armağan
price fiyat
problem sorun, problem
pull (v) çek
pupil öğrenci
push (v) it
put koy
put away kaldır

quality kalite

quarter çeyrek
queue kuyruk
quickly çabuk

radio radyo
rain (v) yağmur
rather oldukça
read (v) oku
ready hazır
receive al
recently yeni
reception resepsiyon
red kırmızı
reliable güvenilir
religion din
remember hatırla
repeat (v) tekrarla, yinele
repetition tekrar
request, ask rica et
reserve (v) ayır
restaurant lokanta, restoran
return, come back dön
rich zengin
right sağ
ring (of bells, etc) (v) çal
road yol, cadde
room oda
rope ip
rose gül
run (v) koş

sad üzgün
salt tuz
salt-cellar tuzluk
same aynı
sand kum
save kurtar
save (money) biriktir
say (v) söyle
school okul
sea deniz
seaside deniz kenarı, kıyı
seat yer
see gör
sell (v) sat
shallow sığ
shirt gömlek
shop dükkan
shopping alışveriş

shops çarşı
shore kıyı
short kısa
shorts şort
shout (v) bağır
show (v) göster
sick hasta
side taraf, yan
sign (v) imzala
signature imza
single (one) tek
single (unmarried) bekâr
sit otur
sky gök, gökyüzü
sleep (n) uyku
sleep (v) uyu
slice dilim
slim zayıf, ince
slow(ly) yavaş
small küçük
smell, scent koku
smoke (n) duman
smoke (v) sigara iç
snow kar
so onun için
soap sabun
soft yumuşak
soldier asker
some bazı
soup çorba
sour ekşi
speak konuş
spectacles gözlük
speech konuşma
speed hız
speedy hızlı
spokesman sözcü
stairs merdiven
stamp pul
star yıldız
start (v) başla
station istasyon
stay (v) kal
stop (v) dur
store mağaza
strange tuhaf
strawberry çilek
street sokak
strength güç, kuvvet

202

strike (n) grev
student öğrenci
study (v) çalış
suddenly birden
sugar şeker
suitcase bavul
sun güneş
surprise (n) sürpriz
surprised, be (v) şaşır
sweet tatlı
swim (v) yüz

table masa
take (v) al
take (time) sür
take along/away götür
talk (v) konuş
tall uzun
taste (of food) (v) lezzet
taxi taksi
tea çay
teacher öğretmen
telephone (n) telefon
telephone (v) telefon et
television televizyon
tell söyle
thank teşekkür et
that şu
these bunlar
thick kalın
thick (in consistency) koyu
thief hırsız
thin zayıf, ince
thing şey
things eşya
think (v) düşün
think (suppose) san
this bu
those şunlar
thousand bin
throw (v) at
ticket bilet
time zaman
tired yorgun
today bugün
tomorrow yarın
top üst
tour tur
tourist turist

towel havlu
town kent, şehir
toy oyuncak
train (n) tren
travel (v) seyahat et
tray tepsi
tree ağaç
trust (v) güven
Turkish (person) Türk
Turkish (language) Türkçe
tyre lastik

ugly çirkin
umbrella şemsiye
under alt
underground train metro
understand anla
upward yukarı

vacate boşalt
valuable değerli, kıymetli
vase vazo
vegetable sebze
very çok
village köy
vine asma

wait (v) bekle
waiter garson
walk (n) yürüyüş
walk (v) yürü
wall duvar
want (v) iste
warm ılık
warn uyar
warning uyarı
wash (v) yıka
watch (n) saat
watch (v) seyret
water su
way yol
weather hava
week hafta
weekend hafta sonu
well iyi
what ne
when ne zaman
where nerede
which hangi

whisky viski
white beyaz
who kim
whose kimin
why neden, niçin
wide geniş
wife karı
win (*v*) kazan
window pencere
wine şarap
winter kış
wish (*n*) dilek
wish (*v*) dile, iste
woman kadın

word kelime
work (*n*) iş
work (*v*) çalış
world dünya
write yaz
wrong yanlış

year yıl, sene
yellow sarı
yes evet
yesterday dün
yet daha, henüz
young genç
young person genç

Index

The numbers refer to section headings

205